Angels

Angels

Traditions, Stories, & Miracles

ISABELLA ANDERSON

AVON, MASSACHUSETTS

Published by
Adams Media, a division of F+W Media, Inc.
57 Littlefield Street, Avon, MA 02322. U.S.A.
www.adamsmedia.com

Contains material adapted from *The Everything® Angels Book* by M.J. Abadie, copyright © 2000 by F+W Media, Inc., ISBN 10: 1-58062-398-0, ISBN 13: 978-1-58062-398-8 and *The Everything® Guide to Angels* by Karen Paolino, CHT, ATP, copyright © 2009 by F+W Media, Inc., ISBN 10: 1-60550-121-2, ISBN 13: 978-1-60550-121-5.

ISBN 10: 1-4405-9510-0
ISBN 13: 978-1-4405-9510-3
eISBN 10: 1-4405-9511-9
eISBN 13: 978-1-4405-9511-0

Printed in the United States of America.

10   9   8   7   6   5   4   3   2   1

Cover images © Clipart.com.
Interior art © iStockphoto.com and Dover Publications.

This book is available at quantity discounts for bulk purchases.
For information, please call 1-800-289-0963.

Contents

INTRODUCTION

*No, I never saw an angel, but it is irrelevant whether
I saw one or not. I feel their presence around me.*

—PAULO COELHO

f you believe in angels, you have plenty of company. According to a recent Associated Press survey, 77 percent of Americans believe that angels exist. Look around you—they're everywhere. Women wear angel charms, babies sport "little angel" T-shirts, cherubs are featured in home décor shops, and just about everyone knows someone with a tattoo of angel wings. Angels have a large role in our popular culture. They're featured in movies like *It's a Wonderful Life*, *City of Angels*, and even *Angels in the Outfield*. Angels interact with humans in popular book series including The Mortal Instruments, Halo, and Fallen. Pop music especially reflects our fascination with these heavenly creatures. It's estimated that one in every thirty pop songs refers to an angel.

Celestial beings are found in just about every religion and culture. Ancient Egyptians believed that every person had a *ka*, a kind of supernatural alter ego. Winged spirits are part of the mythology of many civilizations. Valkyries in Norse mythology carried slain warriors to Valhalla. Persian *fereshta* and Hindu *apsaras* were angelic forces associated with the afterlife. The Old Testament is full of angels acting as guardians, messengers, and even warriors. The archangels, including Michael, Raphael, and Gabriel, were not passive ethereal creatures. They served in God's army—and they were fierce!

While angels have long been loved as symbols of heaven, all-seeing guardians, and heralds of the Christmas season, recently the idea of angel communication has become increasingly popular. There are angel boutiques, angel coaches, and angel card readings—all to help people get in touch with angels. This divine communication can be done in a variety of ways—through meditation, journaling, affirmations, and chanting.

Part Two of this book is dedicated to helping you to connect with the angels. You will learn how to open yourself up to receive divine messages and gain insight into different aspects of your life. You'll discover the magic of signs, synchronicities, and coincidences and learn how to interpret their meaning as messages from angels. Angels can help you release worry, gain patience, let go of guilt, and live in the present moment with a positive attitude. And they will help you to heal physically and emotionally, find a soul mate, enhance relationships, create prosperity, find the perfect job, and manifest your dreams.

So get ready for a magical ride. Open your heart—invite the angels into your life—and expect miracles!

Angels, in the early morning

May be seen the Dews among,

Stooping—plucking—smiling—flying—

Do the Buds to them belong?

Angels, when the sun is hottest

May be seen the sands among,

Stooping—plucking—sighing—flying—

Parched the flowers they bear along.

—EMILY DICKINSON, "ANGELS, IN THE EARLY MORNING"

PART ONE

The

Angelic
Realm

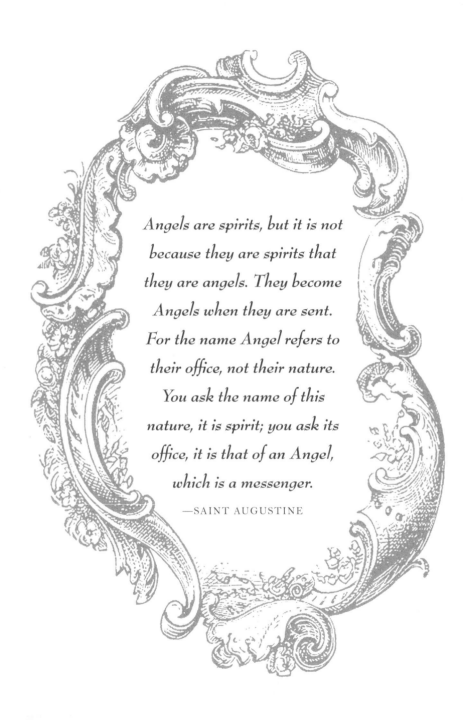

Angels are spirits, but it is not because they are spirits that they are angels. They become Angels when they are sent. For the name Angel refers to their office, not their nature. You ask the name of this nature, it is spirit; you ask its office, it is that of an Angel, which is a messenger.

—SAINT AUGUSTINE

CHAPTER ONE

Ancient Angels

t is unknown if the idea of angels arose in different cultures independently, if the idea traveled from culture to culture, or which cultural ideas seeded the beliefs of others. For thousands of years, merchants and mercenaries, wise men and priests, prophets and pagans, and those uprooted by famine or war have wandered and intermingled. Thus it is that you can find the concept of angels in the mythologies of nearly every known ancient culture. Their appearance and purpose may vary throughout the world and its history, but their universal influence over mankind is a presence of love and guidance, and a reminder that we are not alone.

THE EARLIEST ANGELS

Angels have been recorded in history by many different cultures throughout the world. Some scholars say that the earliest religious representation of angels dates back to the city of Ur, in the Euphrates Valley, c. 4000–2500 B.C.E. A *stele*, which is a stone slab, showed a winged figure descending from one of the seven heavens to pour the water of life from an overflowing jar into a cup held by the king. Other records show that in Mesopotamia there were giant, winged creatures—part human, part animal—known as griffins. And in Egypt, Nephthys, the twin sister of the goddess Isis, is shown in paintings and reliefs enfolding the dead in her beautiful wings.

Without doubt, based upon archeological evidence and other prehistoric information, angels were depicted long before

HERMES, MESSENGER OF THE GODS

Christianity appeared on the religious stage. Descriptions of angels are ancient, predating even early Judaism. Images of angels appear all over Asia Minor, in different cultures of the ancient civilized world, and westward into Greece and Italy. Iris and Hermes, messenger of the gods and guide of souls, both wear wings and serve angelic functions such as carrying messages and bringing aid to humans. The famous Greek sculpture of Nike, The Winged Victory of Samothrace, served as a model for the angels depicted in Renaissance art, firmly establishing the concept of angels in that period.

THE MESSENGERS

The word *angelos* in the original Greek means "messenger," and in this respect, angels may be related to the function of Hermes, one of whose daughters is called "angel" by Pindar. A daughter of Zeus, Iris, the "goddess of the rainbow," is also described as an angel by the writer Hesiod. Such terms suggest that an angel is a special carrier of messages from the gods, an idea that permeates the writings about angels of many cultures.

IRIS, GODDESS OF THE RAINBOW

Winged spirits—angels—
are part of the mystery of
every culture. . . . The Vikings
called them valkyeries. The Greeks
called them horae. In Persia they
were fereshta, and sometimes they were
confused with peri or horis, which are sexless (yes) female celestial
beings who give sensual delight to the inhabitants of Paradise; or with
the Hindu apsaras, the beautiful fairies of heaven who dispensed
sensual and erotic bliss to the gods, though later (especially Christian)
teachings insist that angels are without carnal desire, . . . Still, in
those early Indo-European myths, angels could have children, which
sprouted like cabbages on their laps, already five years old at birth.

—SOPHY BURNHAM, *A BOOK OF ANGELS*

In addition to Hermes (who wore wings on his heels) and Iris (who is often pictured with small wings on her back) from the Greek tradition, there are angel-like figures—often called griffins—in many ancient cultures. Kneeling beside an Etruscan tombstone dating from about 100 B.C.E. are two enormous stone figures with great wings springing from their shoulders. Sometimes griffins were entirely human in appearance, as is the case of the two winged genii depicted on a cylinder seal from Assyria (c. 700–600 B.C.E.) who are thought to be fertilizing the Tree of Life. But even these remarkable representations are recent when compared to the figures from ancient Egypt, Mesopotamia, and Persia.

EGYPTIAN GUARDIANS

In ancient Egypt, the goddess Nepthys, considered along with Isis and Osiris to be one of the progenitors of the world, often appears as a winged figure. Her image is found carved on the inner right-hand door of Shrine III in the tomb of Tutankhamun, c. fourteenth century B.C.E. Tall and erect, she spreads her slender arms, to which her intricately carved wings are attached, in a sweeping motion forward, as if to encompass the dead pharaoh and protect him from all harm.

The ancient Egyptians also believed that each person had a supernatural double, called his or her *ka*, who was born alongside the person and remained a part of his or her life ever after. In one sense, the *ka* was what we today call a guardian angel, but it also represents the soul, or that part of the human being that is able to separate from the body and travel around on its own. The old

Egyptians would have found nothing unusual about what we now refer to as "out of body experiences." Instead, they would have said that their *ka* was simply off somewhere else, unattached to the body.

When the Angels arrive, the devils leave.
—EGYPTIAN PROVERB

Other early cultures depicted winged lions and bulls with human heads who warded off evil and stood between the realm of the myriad gods of the era and their human worshippers.

THE TRANSFORMATION OF ANGELS

Angels are also found in the Asian cultures represented by Buddhism and Taoism. The angels of ancient Assyria and Mesopotamia were a tradition carried down through Manichaean, Judaic, Christian, and Islamic lore, each of which influenced the others' faith in angels. The concept of angels was widely accepted in Asia Minor and extended into the Mediterranean basin of Greece and Italy, where it would become embraced and transformed.

HOW MANY ANGELS ARE THERE?

Angels appear in both the Old and New Testaments, where they are mentioned directly or indirectly about three hundred times. According to David in Psalm 68:17, "the chariots of God are twenty thousand, even thousands of angels." Some biblical scholars believe that angels can be numbered in the millions, based on the comment in Hebrews 12:22, which refers to "an innumerable company of angels."

In Greece, the idea of angels transformed into the famous depiction of Nike in The Winged Victory of Samothrace. During the Renaissance, the once fierce *cherubim* changed from the awesome beings of Ezekiel's vision—terrifying creatures with swords of fire who guarded the Garden of Eden against the return of the expelled Adam and Eve—into *putti*, or cute little pink baby cherubs. Childlike in form and appearance, cherubs usually floated like little Cupids around beautiful, serene women, who are often pregnant or with small children.

THE WINGED VICTORY

SHAMANISM

One of the world's oldest religious traditions, Shamanism, as practiced by some Native Americans, incorporates communication with winged beings. These often come in the form of eagles, ravens, or spirits and are not usually associated with later angelic iconography.

I looked up at the clouds, and two men were coming there, headfirst like arrows slanting down; and as they came, they sang a sacred song and the thunder was like drumming. I will sing it for you. The song and the drumming were like this: "Behold a sacred voice is calling you; All over the sky a sacred voice is calling."

—NICHOLAS BLACK ELK, AS TOLD THROUGH
JOHN G. NEIHARDT IN *BLACK ELK SPEAKS*

Among Native Americans, great birds—Raven and Eagle—were believed to help humans, to heal or bring fire, or to carry messages from God. In this tradition, too, friendly spirits, or familiars, walk among the people and guard them from harm. These winged creatures are considered to be of great help to the tribal shaman in his work.

ANGELS: A COMMON THREAD

We can't ever know if the idea of angels arose in different cultures independently, if the idea traveled from culture to culture, or which cultural ideas seeded those of others. All over Asia, from Byzantium to Cathay, for thousands of years, merchants and mercenaries, wise men and priests, prophets and pagans, and those uprooted by famine or war wandered and intermingled. The angel concept courses through the centuries like a single thread on which each culture hung its own variations of the same theme.

When a man dies, they who survive him ask what property he has left behind. The angel who bends over the dying man asks what good deeds he has sent before him.

—THE KORAN

For he shall give his angels
charge over thee to keep
thee in all thy ways.

—PSALM 91:11

CHAPTER TWO

Angels in the Old Testament

everal angels appear in stories throughout the Old Testament. In the earlier books, the angels are described as heavenly beings created by God. As religious beliefs transformed throughout the ages, so too did the view of the angels. There were angels who brought news of death and destruction and others who killed thousands. There were also stories in the Bible about ministering angels who provided protection and comfort, and delivered words of wisdom from God.

ABRAHAM AND SARAH

In Genesis 16 and 21, angels are introduced in an amazingly dramatic scenario that could have come from a Hollywood production. Imagine the following: a young woman, Hagar, became pregnant by an important man with a powerful wife, Sarah, who was infertile. The unfortunate girl was in a most inferior position, lower even than a servant; she was a slave. And it was the wife herself who had presented the girl as a gift—a concubine—to her husband, Abraham.

Sarah was less than pleased to find that the concubine was impregnated with her husband's seed. In fact, Sarah made Hagar's life a living hell. When the poor girl could take no more abuse, she ran away. At this time, of course, there were no women's shelters, only the wilderness, full of wild beasts and all manner of other dangers. And Hagar had no money, though money wouldn't have helped much in any case.

During her flight, she found a spring on the road to Shur and stopped there to rest and refresh herself. Here she had the first of two encounters with angelic presences, called holy ones by the Jews. According to Genesis 16:7–11, "the angel of the Lord found her . . . and said to her, 'Return to your mistress, and submit yourself to her authority [for] you are with child, and you shall bear a son; and you shall call his name Ishmael.'"

Not knowing what else to do, Hagar obeyed the angel and returned to Abraham's house and gave birth to a boy, naming him Ishmael as she had been directed. Hagar and her son were soon cast out into the desert (Genesis 21:14–19), and Ishmael was dying

HAGAR AND ISMAEL IN THE WILDERNESS
(GIOVANNI BATTISTA TIEPOLO, C. 1732)

of thirst. Fearful for her son's life, Hagar prayed as she had been taught to do; as she did, she heard the voice she had heard earlier:

> *"'What is the matter with you, Hagar? Do not fear, for God has heard the voice of the lad where he is,'" said the voice of the angel of God, and Hagar took heart hearing this call from heaven.*
>
> *"Then God opened her eyes and she saw a well of water; and she went and filled the skin with water, and gave the lad a drink. And God was with the lad."*

Abraham, too, entertained angels, as we are told in Genesis, but these appeared as ordinary men. They came and sat down to dinner with Abraham and Sarah. As the angels were departing, they informed Sarah that she would bear a child, a son named Isaac, whose descendants would found a great Hebrew nation. It was this startling announcement, considering the circumstances of the aged couple, that made Abraham realize he had been visited by holy ones, or angels.

ISAIAH ON ANGELS

"Anyone who doubts [the grandeur of angels] should read a first-hand description of angels as they were in Old Testament times, such as what Isaiah said of these heavenly creatures:

"'In the year that king Uzziah died I saw also the Lord sitting upon a throne, high and lifted up, and his train filled the temple. Above it stood the seraphims: each one had six wings; with twain he covered his face, and with twain he covered his feet, and with twain he did fly.'"

"Another passage comments that every seraph has four faces . . . There is a Syrian depiction in sculpture of a demon that exactly meets Isaiah's standards; it dates from the eighth century B.C.E. It has six wings, holds a serpent in each hand, and is terrifying. . . . Some scholars have pointed out that the Hebrew *saraph*, possibly the origin of the word 'seraph,' means 'serpent.' Seraphim is translated as 'burning ones.' . . . but let us return to Isaiah:

"'And one cried unto another, and said, Holy, holy, holy, is the Lord of hosts: the whole earth is full of His glory. And the posts of the door moved at the voice of him that cried, and the house was filled with smoke. Then said I, Woe is me! . . . Then flew one of the seraphims unto me, having a live coal in his hand, which he had taken with the tongs from off the altar: And he laid it upon my mouth, and said, Lo, this hath touched thy lips; and thine iniquity is taken away, and thy sin is purged.'"

—Emily Hahn, *Breath of God*

JACOB WRESTLING WITH THE ANGEL

JACOB

Abraham's grandson, Jacob, had a difficult experience with an angel, wrestling with him all night in the dark. He hadn't a clue who his adversary was, for the angel apparently appeared as an ordinary man without a wing in sight.

As a young man, Jacob had cheated his brother Esau out of his inheritance by deceiving their blind father. He had also tricked his uncle Laban out of all his wealth and possessions, after which he left his family's settlement. Jacob married twice and fathered twelve sons. Later in life, Jacob decided to return home. After what he'd been up to, he wasn't quite sure of his welcome, so he set up camp half-a-day's camel ride from Esau's encampment and began sending gifts—entire herds of sheep and goats, thirty she-camels for milking, along with their young, twenty female asses and their ten offspring, and forty cows just for good measure. Milk was much appreciated in the desert climate.

I will bless the Lord at all times, His praise shall continually be in my mouth. My soul shall make its boast in the Lord; the humble shall hear it and rejoice. O magnify the Lord with me, and let us exalt His name together.

I sought the Lord, and He answered me, and delivered me from all my fears. They looked to Him and were radiant, and their faces shall never be ashamed. This poor man cried and the Lord heard him; and saved him out of all his troubles. The angel of the Lord encamps around those who fear Him, and rescues them.

—PSALM 34:1–7

Even after sending all these elaborate peace offerings, Jacob's mind was not at rest; he knew he'd done wrong. He feared Esau might kill him when he discovered he was nearby. One night, an angel came. Jacob wrestled with the angel all night long, not knowing who his adversary was. In the end, Jacob prevailed. He then demanded a blessing from the angel, who gave it without ever identifying itself. But Jacob figured out that his struggle had been with a supernatural being, and since he had won, he concluded that all would be well with his brother.

The next day he arranged to meet Esau. He took all of his wives, servants, livestock, and other riches, and traveled to where his brother awaited him. Esau arrived with an armed guard of 450 men, but he offered Jacob peace and forgiveness and professed to be glad to be reunited with his brother.

Early Jews contended that the universe was a hierarchy, with God at the top and other entities radiating downward from Him. They believed that angels constitute the "court of heaven." In writings they referred to "the angels of God," and bene Elohim, "God's sons."

—JOAN WESTER ANDERSON, *WHERE ANGELS WALK*

This same Jacob is the one famous for "Jacob's ladder." In a vision, he saw a multitude of angels ascending and descending a ladder that reached up to heaven. The Bible does not report whether the angels in Jacob's vision had wings, but one would presume not, since they were climbing up and down the ladder. None of these angels had any unusual garments or characteristics that would distinguish them from ordinary men. They had no halos (these would be introduced later in medieval art) and wore no "shining garments of the Lord." They were just working angels in plain clothes and nothing more. Such angel visitations are similar to those reportedly made by the Greek gods to favored mortals. Hermes appeared often as a youthful stranger, showing the way or being helpful in some manner.

Jacob was deeply involved with angelic presences all through his life, and when he reached the end of it, he reviewed his experiences with the holy ones. In wonder he exclaimed, "God . . . has been my shepherd all my life to this day, the angel who has redeemed me from all evil."

ABRAHAM AND ISAAC

One of the most famous biblical stories of angels has to do with Abraham and his son Isaac. One day, Abraham heard the voice of God calling to him through an angel. In Genesis 22:11, we are told, "And the angel of the Lord called unto him out of heaven, and said, 'Abraham, Abraham' and he said, 'Here am I.'"

The voice instructed him to sacrifice his son Isaac. It ordered him to take the boy to the top of a remote mountain and slit his throat in the manner of the usual sacrificial lamb and to let his blood run out as an offering to prove to God that Abraham was a true and complete devotee. Giving up that which was most dear to him, his only child, would show God that Abraham's devotion included complete surrender to God's will.

Without questioning this heavenly dictum, Abraham made preparations for a sacrifice, sharpening his knife and gathering wood for a fire. Revealing his aims to no one, not even his wife (one can imagine what might have happened if he had revealed to her God's peculiar message), he took his son and, accompanied by one servant, went off into the wilderness.

BIBLICAL REFERENCES
TO ANGELS' DUTIES

Isaiah 6:2 speaks of the six-winged seraphim as distinct from cherubim. God is said to be seated above the cherubim in I Samuel 4:4, Psalm 80:1, and Psalm 99:1. However, in Isaiah's vision, the seraphim stood above God. Evidently, the duties of these two orders differ: Cherubim are the guardians of the throne of God and act as God's elite corps of ambassadors; seraphim are charged with the ceaseless worship of God, as well as the purification of His other servants.

Leaving the servant at the bottom of the mountain, Abraham went ahead with the boy, who trustingly expected to help his father sacrifice a lamb.

At one point Isaac realized there wasn't any animal with them and asked, "Father?" to which Abraham answered, as he had to the angel, "Here I am, my son."

ABRAHAM'S SACRIFICE OF ISAAC

The boy said, "We have the knife and wood for the fire, but there is no lamb."

"God will provide," answered Abraham, knowing that God had already provided the sacrificial lamb in the person of his beloved son. At a certain point, Abraham and Isaac built an altar of stone and laid the fire and lit it. When it was going well, Abraham suddenly took hold of the boy and bound him hand and foot. Laying him across the altar, he raised the keen-edged knife in his hand and put it against his son's throat. As he was about to slice into flesh of his flesh, the angel's voice stopped him. "Lay not thy hand upon the lad," commanded the voice. Abraham obeyed, no doubt thankfully, and at that moment, he spotted a sheep with its woolly fleece entangled in the thorns of a bush. He caught it and sacrificed it, offering it up to God in place of his son.

MOSES

For forty years the Israelites were enslaved in Egypt, and the all-powerful Pharaoh refused to free them. Moses, desperate for his people to achieve their freedom, declared: "But when we cried out to the Lord, He heard our voice and sent an angel and brought us out of Egypt" (Numbers 20:16). After having delivered the people of Israel from Egypt and overseen their emancipation from the Pharaoh, the angel did not forsake them. The angel divided the waters of the Red Sea so they could pass through without getting wet. Then when the powerful army of Egypt was in hot pursuit, the "angel of God who had been going before the camp of Israel, moved and went behind them; and the pillar of cloud moved from before them and stood behind them. So it came between the camp of Egypt and the camp of Israel and there was the cloud along with the darkness, yet it gave light at night. Thus the one did not come near the other all night" (Exodus 14:19–20).

ANGEL OF DEATH

The Angel of Death, an agent of destruction, presumably acting under direct orders from God at the time of David, destroyed 90,000 people. On another occasion, in the Assyrian army camp that was arrayed against the Jews, it came along and killed 185,000 of King

Sennacherib's soldiers as he was about to invade Jerusalem. This last was considered to be such a miraculous intervention that it is mentioned at length. Here is one description: "And it came to pass that night, that the angel of the Lord went out, and smote in the camp of the Assyrians a hundred fourscore and five thousand; and when they arose early in the morning, behold, they were all dead corpses" (II Kings 19:35). Not surprisingly, Sennacherib returned home to Nineveh.

THE DESTRUCTION OF THE ARMY OF SENNACHERIB

DANIEL IN THE LION'S DEN

DANIEL

Last, but not least, of Old Testament angelic interventions is the story of Daniel in the lion's den. King Darius, a man who could recognize piety and courage when he saw it, predicted that Daniel's faith would save him from being eaten. He came to Daniel just before he was to be tossed into the den of the starved lions and said, "Your God whom you constantly serve will Himself deliver you."

In the morning, apparently somewhat worried about what might have transpired during Daniel's night with the hungry beast, the king approached the den and called out, "Daniel, servant of the living God, has your God, whom you constantly serve, been able to deliver you from the lions?"

Alive and well, Daniel was able to answer the worried king, saying, "O king, live forever! My God sent His angel [into the den before Daniel got there] and shut the lions' mouths, and they have not harmed me" (Daniel 6:16–23).

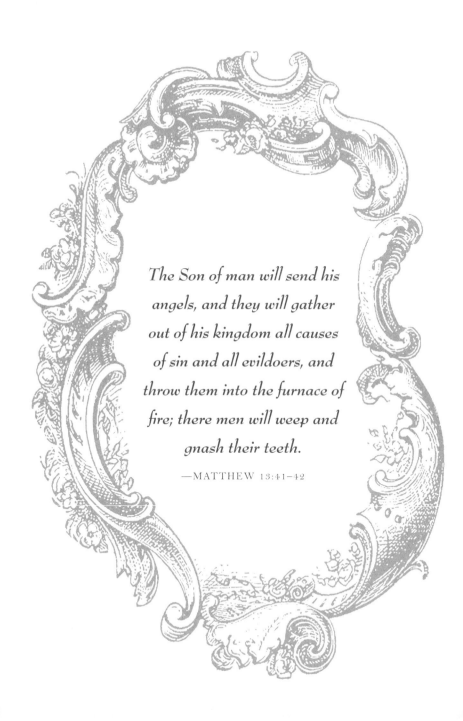

The Son of man will send his angels, and they will gather out of his kingdom all causes of sin and all evildoers, and throw them into the furnace of fire; there men will weep and gnash their teeth.

—MATTHEW 13:41–42

CHAPTER THREE

Christian Angels

he roles of angels change dramatically in the New Testament. Gone are the Angels of Death and Vengeance, and also gone are the heroic deeds of angels. No longer do angels bring death and destruction, nor do they go about killing the firstborn of unbelievers. The physical appearance of angels also changes. In the New Testament, angels are no longer depicted as bland creatures without personalities. They change from being purely abstract extensions of God to being friends with humankind, and have powers that can be called upon in times of stress or need.

THE ANNUNCIATION

Of course, the most important angelic visitation in the view of the early Christians is the Annunciation, the speaking of those famous words: *Ave Maria, gratia plena, Dominus tecum: Hail Mary, full of grace, the Lord is with thee.*

THE ANNUNCIATION (FRA ANGELICO, C. 1430–45)

Although Mary didn't quite understand what the angel meant, she realized the message was of great importance and kept puzzling about its meaning. Then the angel came to her and said, "Do not be afraid, Mary; for you have found favor with God. And behold, you will conceive in your womb, and bear a son, and you shall name him

Jesus. He will be great, and will be called the Son of the Most High; and the Lord God will give Him the throne of His Father David; and He will reign over the house of Jacob forever; and His kingdom will have no end."

In the Christian world . . . it is believed that angels were created at the beginning, and that heaven was formed of them; and that the Devil or Satan was an angel of light, who, becoming rebellious, was cast down with his crew, and that this was the origin of hell.

—EMANUEL SWEDENBORG

When Mary's pregnancy became obvious, Joseph, her husband, who was a much older man, was embarrassed by the situation and wanted to quietly put her away somewhere so that her condition would not cause him and his family shame. But an angel of the Lord appeared to him in a dream, saying, "Joseph, son of David, do not be afraid . . . for that which has been conceived in her is of the Holy Spirit. And she will bear a Son; and you shall call His name Jesus, for it is He who will save His people from their sins."

After the birth of Jesus, the angel of the Lord continued to look after the family's safety. Herod, the Roman-appointed ruler of Jerusalem, heard rumors that the newborn might be a threat, became jealous of the child and what his birth might mean, and made plans to have him killed.

Once again, the angel appeared to Joseph in a dream and warned him, saying, "Arise, and take the Child and His mother, and flee to Egypt, and remain there until I tell you; for Herod is going to search for the Child to destroy Him." Later, after Herod died, the angel appeared again to Joseph in another dream and told him, "Arise, and take the Child and His mother, and go into the land of Israel; for those who sought the Child's life are dead" (Matthew, Chapter 2).

ANGELS AFTER THE CRUCIFIXION OF CHRIST

The Gospel of Matthew mentions that two angels—without wings but with "a countenance like lightning" and "garments white as snow"—were found sitting inside the cave in which Jesus had been laid in burial.

Mary Magdalene and Mary (James's mother) went to the tomb to care for the dead body, but there was no body to be seen anywhere. It had disappeared. One of the angels informed the amazed and startled women that the reason there wasn't a corpse was that Jesus had "risen up from the dead."

Not knowing what to think about this extraordinary occurrence, the women rushed back to where the eleven remaining apostles were waiting and related their story. Naturally, the men were skeptical, but

THE RESURRECTION OF CHRIST

they rushed up the hill to take a look for themselves and indeed found the tomb empty. This story is told in many different versions by different Gospel writers, but the basic elements are the same.

PAUL'S ANGEL

In the New Testament Apocrypha, Paul is guided by an angel on a complicated and confusing journey through the territory of heaven and hell. The narrative shifts back and forth between beauty and horror: He sees hell and several blessed abodes. He has visions of utter bliss, and visions of terrible punishments. The vision provides a wealth of imagery and an interesting role for his angelic guide. Finally, the angel leads Paul to the door of the third heaven. Paul says, "And I looked at it and saw that it was a golden gate and that there were two golden tables above the pillars full of letters. [These letters are the names of the righteous, already inscribed in heaven while they still live on earth.] And again the angel turned to me and said: 'Blessed are you if you enter in by these gates.'"

After entering the gates of paradise, Paul encounters the ancient prophet Enoch, who issues a warning to Paul not to reveal what he has seen in the third heaven. Then, the angel descends, with Paul in tow, to the second heaven and then to the earthly paradise, where the souls of those deemed righteous await the resurrection.

Here, Paul sees the four rivers of paradise, which flow with milk, wine, honey, and olive oil, and on the banks of each river he meets those souls who have exhibited some specific virtue in their lives: The river of milk is for those who are innocent and chaste; the river of wine, a reward for those who have shown hospitality to strangers; the river of honey, for those who have submitted their own will to the will of God; and the river of oil for those who have renounced earthly pleasure and gain for love of God.

The angel puts Paul in a golden boat, and the narrative continues: "And about three thousand angels were singing a hymn before me until I reached the City of Christ."

Sinners who have repented of their crimes are gathered in a forest, where they abide during the time between death and resurrection. The City of Christ is made with twelve walls, each exceeding the one before in greatness, and Paul goes into the center of this apparent maze and says:

> *I saw in the midst of this city a great altar, very high, and there was [David] standing near the altar, whose countenance shone as the sun, and he held in his hands a psaltery and harp, and he sang psalms, saying Alleluia. And all in the city replied Alleluia till the very foundations of the city were shaken. . . . Turning round I saw golden thrones placed in each gate, and on them men having golden diadems and gems: and I looked carefully and saw inside between the twelve men thrones in glorious rank . . . so that no one is able to recount their praise. . . . Those thrones belong to those who had goodness and understanding of heart and made themselves fools for the sake of the Lord God.*

Paul is occupied looking at the trees of heaven when he sees two hundred angels preceding Mary and singing hymns. Mary informs him that he has been granted the unusual favor of coming to this place before he is dead.

ISAIAH'S ANGEL

The story of the Ascension of Isaiah (in the New Testament Apocrypha) is far less complex. The prophet is taken out of his body and led by an angel to the first heaven above the sky: "And I saw a throne in the midst, and on the right and on the left of it were angels [singing praises]." He asks whom they praise, and is told by the angels, "It is for the praise of him who is in the seventh heaven, for him who rests in eternity among his saints, and for his Beloved, whence I have been sent unto [you]."

The "heaven above the sky" is the first heaven (of seven), and the angel then takes Isaiah to the second heaven, where once more he

ISAIAH'S VISION

sees, as before, a throne and angels to the right and to the left. Awed by the situation, the holy prophet prostrates himself to worship the angel on the throne (there is some confusion here about a throne being an angel and an angel being on a throne) but is told not to do that. Angels are not to be worshiped.

Ascending further, each of the succeeding heavens is filled with more glory than the one before, and the sixth heaven is of such glorious brightness that it makes the previous five dark by comparison. Naturally—in common with those who have reported near-death experiences—Isaiah wants to remain in this place of wonders and not be sent back to a dull life encased in earthly flesh. But the angel explains that Isaiah's time on earth isn't finished: "If [you] already rejoice in this light, how much [will you] rejoice when, in the seventh heaven, [you see] that light where God and his beloved are, whence I have been sent. . . . As for [your] wish not to return to the flesh . . . [your] days are not yet fulfilled that [you may] come here."

Isaiah is saddened, but Jesus himself allows Isaiah to enter the seventh heaven, of which he reports: "And I saw there a wonderful light and angels without number. And there I saw all the righteous from Adam . . . I saw Enoch and all who were with him stripped of the garment of the flesh, and I saw them in their higher garments, and they were like the angels who stand there in great glory."

The vision ends with Jesus escorting Isaiah down through all the heavens to earth to witness the Annunciation and the Incarnation.

THE CHRISTIAN CHURCH'S VIEW ON ANGELS

Constantine the Great, who was the emperor of Byzantium (306–337), converted to Christianity after having a powerful vision of a cross in the sky. It was profound enough to cause him to convert even though Christianity was still a minority religion. His conversion convinced many others to follow. During this time period he also declared that angels have wings.

CHAPTER THREE: CHRISTIAN ANGELS

No doubt Constantine had a lot to do with the renewed interest in angels. At that time most people were used to stories of fairies and it was a small stretch from a winged fairy to an angel with wings.

What concerned the church fathers was that the common people were worshiping angels, and they believed that only God and His Son could be worshiped. This dilemma had been settled by St. Paul when he attacked and denied the worship of angels with his usual "I know what's best here" attitude. Nevertheless, the First Council of Nicaea in 325 decided that belief in angels was to be church dogma. Apparently, this decision unleashed a rampant renewal of the angel worship that St. Paul had so detested. In 343, less than twenty years after Nicaea, the worship of angels was proclaimed idolatry by another council.

NAMES OF ANGELS

By the fifth century, there were so many angels' names that a riot of confusion set in, causing the Church to declare that only seven angels, the archangels, are to be known by name. In line with the usual disputation about angels, only four of these—Raphael, Michael, Gabriel, and Uriel—remain constant throughout all the various systems. At the Ad Lateran Synod of 745, the active practice of giving names to angels was condemned. The good fathers worried that if angels all had names, angel worship would become a problem (it might hearken back to the pagan way of naming all sorts of spirits, both celestial and natural), so they decreed there should be no more naming of angels, in order that only God would be worshiped.

Finally, in 787, to end the controversy, the second Council of Nicaea, called the Seventh Ecumenical Synod, was held. It declared a limited dogma of the archangels, which included their names, their specific functions, and also formally legitimated the depiction of angels in art.

THE JEWISH TRADITION

While all the debate about angels was going on in the predominantly Christian world of Europe, a Jewish population lived alongside their Christian neighbors yet remained totally isolated from them. It's hard to see how any metaphysical or theological ideas might have been exchanged between the two communities, with one clearly superior in number and political clout. Thus separated, and trying to maintain their own identity as a people through their language and traditional culture, medieval Jews lived in religious isolation.

AN ARMY OF ANGELS

In the Jewish Kabbalah, the number of angels is listed at 49 million, while by another count there are 496,000 angels, ranked into seven divisions like an army. In a vision, Daniel saw that "thousands of thousands ministered to him and ten thousand times a hundred thousand stood before him."

The Kabbalah (also seen as *Kabala, Kabbala, Cabala, Cabalah*) is the great book of the Jewish religion. The term Kabbalah is derived from the Hebrew root *kbl*, which means "to receive." It refers to matters that are occult (meaning "hidden") or mystical knowledge so secret that it is rarely written down. It is transmitted from master to neophyte, or student, orally, in order to protect the secrets from being revealed to those not prepared to receive them or unworthy to do so.

All of the books of the Kabbalah constitute a system of guidance to the path to God, on which the believer is taken through a series of heavenly halls guided by angels. It is replete with long descriptions of how to make the journey safely up through a tree of angels, and it gives the secret passwords to bypass demons encountered along the path.

In the Kabbalah are ten sefirot, or angels, considered to be the fundamental channels of divine energy. Their names are Foundation, Splendor, Eternity, Beauty, Power, Grace, Knowledge, Wisdom, Understanding, and Crown. They are arranged in the shape of a tree and called the Tree of Life. The top of this tree is occupied by the singular angel Keter, and beyond all of this is the mystical contemplation of God. It is so distant and removed that it makes it incomprehensible to ever know God directly, but only experience Him through His angels.

As you can see, the angels play an important role in the teachings of the Kabbalah. They once again act as intermediaries between heaven and earth and oversee what occurs on earth.

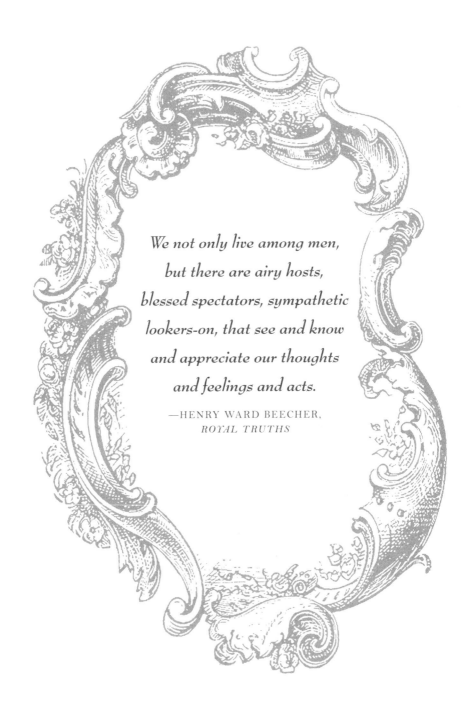

We not only live among men,
but there are airy hosts,
blessed spectators, sympathetic
lookers-on, that see and know
and appreciate our thoughts
and feelings and acts.

—HENRY WARD BEECHER,
ROYAL TRUTHS

CHAPTER FOUR

What Is an Angel?

here are many interpretations available to answer the question, What is an angel? The narratives in early books of Scripture portray angels as mere extensions of God, emotionless and featureless. But later texts indicate they are capable of feelings and have individual personalities. For example, the angel who wrestles with Jacob and the angel who foretells of Samson's birth and mission both refuse to identify themselves. These angels lack personality and warmth; they seem more like robotic minions sent to carry out a job. However, more personalized images of angels are found later, such as the stories about Michael and his special duties, or Luke's narrative about Gabriel and Mary.

ENERGY AND LIGHT

Originally, angels were not described in any one particular way, neither in form nor appearance, nor in function. Says G. Don Gilmore in *Angels, Angels, Everywhere*: "An angel is a form through which a specific essence or energy force can be transmitted for a specific purpose."

The more we study how angels are, or were, perceived by different cultures, the more infinitely variable they become. For example, the Gnostics, who were influenced by Persian traditions, believed that angels lived in a world of mystical light between the mundane world and the "Transcendent Causeless Cause"; in other words, between heaven and earth.

Despite the different ideas about how they looked and what they were, angels were part of people's everyday life until the Middle Ages. But their influence upon the general populace began to wane after the thirteenth century. With the coming of Protestantism, angels took a back seat; Protestants had no need of intermediaries between themselves and God. In fact, that was one of the main reasons for getting rid of Catholicism, so that the individual worshipper could contact God directly without having to go through a priest or other intermediary, including the Virgin Mary and angels.

Although the great Renaissance painters depicted angels as fluffy, friendly winged creatures and as adorable little cherubs floating about the heads of beautiful women with cute children on their laps, angels lost their previous importance for everyday folk. And by the time of the Enlightenment—with its emphasis on science and rational thought—angels had been relegated to the level of fairies (the stuff of poetry, romantic fancy, and children's stories).

Christians believe that God made angels at or about the time He made the world (Saint Augustine thought the two acts of creation were simultaneous), but before He created human beings. They were given minds and wills, like us, but had no bodies. At some point, according to the Book of Revelation, some of the angels wished to be gods and there was a terrible battle in heaven. The defeated angels then became evil spirits, headed by Satan, who roam the world to this day.

—JOAN WESTER ANDERSON, *WHERE ANGELS WALK*

DIVINE MESSENGERS

The word "angel" is derived from the Greek *angelos*, which comes from the Hebrew *mal'akh*, translated literally as "messenger," and the Latin *angelus*, also translated as "messenger." Other roots for the word "angel" come from *angiras* (Sanskrit), meaning "a divine spirit," and from *angaros*, a Persian word meaning "courier," another term for "messenger."

However, the image of the angel as messenger, which is the most common that we have, limits angels considerably. From earliest times, angels were never seen as single-purpose beings, even though they did carry out messenger duties.

In the original languages of the Old and New Testaments, the words translated angel literally and simply to mean messenger. And this is how we most often find angels at work in the Bible: carrying a message. When they poke their celestial heads into stories of the Bible, more often than not it is to say something, guide a wandering nation, trumpet astonishing news, or set somebody straight.

—TIMOTHY JONES, *CELEBRATION OF ANGELS*

As angelology was originally developed in ancient Persia, from where it was absorbed into Judaism and Christianity, and as the medieval church was extremely disputatious as to what exactly an angel *is*, there is considerable latitude available to the modern person in answering the question, What is an angel?

*Whatever **you** think an angel is* might just be the right answer. For people today continue to experience angels through visions, dreams, and meditative states—or altered states of consciousness—just as they have throughout history.

EARLY DESCRIPTIONS

No single description fits all angels. As you've learned, biblical accounts tell of angels appearing as ordinary men, or as radiant light, or dressed in shining white garb. Some have wings, some don't. Angels with wings only occasionally appear in the Bible. Generally speaking, wings were a later addition, dating from the conversion of Constantine the Great.

However, you'll recall one early description of winged angels. The Old Testament prophet Isaiah described seraphim. These angels stand above the throne of God and are awesome indeed. They have lots of wings—six of them in fact. Two are used to cover their faces, some say against the glory of God, others for shame at human sinfulness. Another two wings were used to cover their feet in a reverential gesture (because they *stand* before the Highest Holy of Holies). The third pair of wings was used for flying, according them swiftness in delivering God's messages.

Because He is love in its essence, God appears before the angels . . . as a sun. And from that sun, heat and light go forth; the heat being love and the light, wisdom. And the angels [become] love and wisdom, not from themselves but from the Lord."

—EMANUEL SWEDENBORG, *ANGELIC WISDOM*

The biblical story of Adam and Eve describes the cherubim, whom God placed at the east end of the Garden of Eden to keep Adam and Eve from returning to eat the fruit of the second tree, the Tree of Immortal Life: "Cherubim, and a flaming sword which turned every way, to keep the way of the tree of life."

In later medieval symbolism, seraphim are shown as red, with three pairs of wings, and carrying swords of fire, emblematic of their duty to inflame the hearts of humans with love of God.

HALOS AND WINGS

Toward the end of the fourth century, angels acquired halos, and it wasn't long before a halo became regulation attire for angelic appearances, especially in paintings and stained glass windows in

AN ANGEL WITH WINGS AND HALO

churches. This is despite the fact that the word *halo* doesn't even appear in the Bible, and in which there is nothing to suggest that angels possess them. However, since the halo is a great symbol to suggest out-of-the-ordinary beings and holiness (the Virgin Mary usually wears a halo as well), and since biblical angel appearances often involve the effect of radiant light, the halo makes sense.

THE END OF WINGLESS ANGELS

The wingless angels seen in the tomb of Christ soon sprouted wings, superseding the literal gospel account of how angels appeared to humans. Wings became a distinguishing characteristic of angels, making them easy to recognize as such.

Wings feature as standard equipment for angels especially after the Renaissance period, during which the great painter Raphael and others displayed angels with enormous feathery wings and benign countenances, marking the beginning of the era of the "nice" angel.

ARCHANGELS

The names of angels are numerous. The least bit of research into this subject reveals not dozens but hundreds of recorded names of angels, and variations of the names of different angels. For example, the archangel Raziel is also known as Akraziel, Saraqael, Suriel, Galisur, N'Zuriel, and Uriel. The seraph Semyaza's variations are Samiaza, Shemhazai, Amezyarak, Azael, Azaziel, and Uzza.

Metatron had a mystery name—Bizbul—but he had over a hundred other names as well.

In Hebrew terms and lore, there are seven heavens, as well as seven archangels:

1. The first heaven is called Shamayim, and it is ruled over by Gabriel.
2. The second heaven is called Raqia, co-ruled by Zachariel and Raphael. Raphael is considered to be a great healing angel in the Near East.
3. The third heaven is called Shehaqim, whose chief ruler is Anahel. The Garden of Eden with its Tree of Life is found in the third heaven.
4. The fourth heaven is called Machonon, and its ruler is Michael. One of the oldest shrines in Turkey is dedicated to Michael, whom the Turkish people consider to be a great healer.
5. The fifth heaven is called Mathey, ruled by Sandalphon.
6. The sixth heaven is called Zebul, and it has three rulers. The main ruler is Zachiel, who has two subordinates, Zebul, who rules during the day, and Sabath, who rules the night.
7. The seventh heaven is called Araboth, and it is ruled by Cassiel.

Other texts reference different names and realms, but most mention the four most popular archangels: Michael, Gabriel, Raphael, and Uriel.

Michael

Michael ("who is as God") ranks as the greatest of all angels, whether in Jewish, Christian, or Islamic lore and writings. Michael is chief of the order of virtues, chief of archangels, prince of the presence (of God), angel of repentance, righteousness, mercy, and sanctification. In early times, he was also the guardian of Jacob and the conqueror of Satan, who was still alive and well and causing mischief among humans.

Michael's "mystery name" is *Sabbathiel*, and in Islamic texts, his name is Mika'il. He has been described as the angel who destroyed the armies of Sennacherib (but this feat has also been credited to Gabriel, Uriel, and Ramiel, so take your choice). Michael is supposed to be the angel who stayed Abraham's knife-wielding hand at the throat of his young son Isaac, forbidding the sacrifice of the child. (This deliverance has also been described as the work of other angels, especially Tadhiel and Metatron.) In Jewish lore, Michael is identified as the burning bush that guided Moses in the desert. Talmudic comment Berakot 35, on Genesis 18:1–10, claims that Michael was one of the three "men" who visited Sarah to announce she would have a child.

Michael has also been equated with the Holy Ghost and the third part of the Trinity; early Muslim tradition places Michael in the seventh heaven, with brilliant green wings the color of emeralds. To Christians, St. Michael is the benevolent angel of death, delivering the souls of the faithful to the immortal realm and the eternal light.

Michael was heard by Joan of Arc. According to the court testimony at her trial, Michael inspired the Maid of Orleans to raise

St. Michael (Bartolomé Estéban Murillo, c.1665–66)

an army and go to the aid of the dauphin of France, who became Charles VII largely due to Joan raising the siege of Orleans.

ORIGINS OF THE SEVEN ARCHANGELS

The number seven is an ancient symbolic number. There were seven Akkadian elemental spirits or deities, which may have been protypical of later cultures having seven rulers or creators in their cosmological systems. These are given as *An* (heaven); *Gula* (earth); *Ud* (sun); *Im* (storm); *Istar*, also *Ishtar* (moon); *Ea* or *Dara* (ocean); and *En-lil* (hell). It has been suggested by some that the original models of the seven archangels were the moon and six planets (the three outer planets, Uranus, Neptune, and Pluto, were discovered only recently). All of the planets were Babylonian deities.

Gabriel

Gabriel ("God is my strength") is the second highest ranking angel in the literature of all three of the major monotheistic religions—Judaism, Christianity, and Islam. The angel of annunciation, resurrection, mercy, vengeance, death, and revelation, he is an extremely busy angel with status to match. In Midrash *Eleh Ezkerah*, for example, Gabriel is a major figure in the tale of the ten martyrs (Jewish savants). One of these, Rabbi Ishmael, travels to heaven to inquire of Gabriel why they must die. He is told that they must atone for the sin of the ten sons of Jacob, who sold Joseph into slavery.

ANGEL OF JUDGMENT, ANGEL OF MERCY

In the Judaic tradition, Gabriel was the Angel of Judgment, and he could be fierce indeed. However, under the aegis of Christianity, he became transformed into the Angel of Mercy. Such is the power of religious revision of history!

In addition to having been the angel of the annunciation to Mary of her impending pregnancy, Gabriel presides over Paradise. As the ruling prince of the first heaven, he is said to sit on the left-hand side of God. (Presumably, Michael, who is a bit higher in importance, sits at the right-hand side of God, although this position is later given to Mary upon her assumption into heaven.)

Mohammed claimed that Gabriel—or Jibril in Islamic—was the angel who dictated the Koran to him. Mohammedans consider Gabriel to be the spirit of truth. Jewish legend views Gabriel as an angel of death and destruction to sinful cities, Sodom and Gomorrah being especially vivid examples of this angelic fury. And Talmudic lore has it that Gabriel was the angel who smote the armies of Sennacherib "with a sharpened scythe which had been ready since Creation" (Sanhedrin 95b).

THE ANNUNCIATION (LORENZO DI CREDI, C. 1480–85)

Raphael

Raphael ("God has healed") is known as the healer, not only of humans but of earth itself. His first appearance is in Tobit. Raphael guides Tobit's son Tobias on a journey from Nineveh to Media, acting as a companion. At the end of the trek, the angel reveals himself by name as one of the seven holy angels who stand at God's throne in heaven.

Raphael is a seraph who is also the head of all the guardian angels. He is also known as the Angel of Providence, and in that capacity he watches over all of humanity. This is an extension of his supervisory capacity of the guardian angels, each of whom looks after only one human. He is a sort of angelic CEO of the Guardian Angel Division.

RAPHAEL AND THE DEMON WORKERS

The dossier of Raphael is an inexhaustible file. But one legend stands out; it is taken from the Testament of Solomon. Solomon prays to God for assistance in the building of the temple, and his prayer is answered in the gift of a magical ring, delivered to the Hebrew king personally by Raphael. This ring was engraved with a pentagram—a five-pointed star—and it had the power to summon and control demons. So it was with this God-given demon-labor (free of charge, naturally) that King Solomon completed the building of the great temple. It may be from this tale that we get the common expression, "working like a demon."

As one who accompanies travelers, Raphael is related to the Greek god Mercury, the patron god of travel and all communications. As usual, these attributes are derived from a long line of historical and mythological connotations that have come down through the ages.

Raphael is especially concerned with pilgrims traveling to some holy site or, metaphysically speaking, on the path toward God. Thus, he is seen walking with a staff, wearing sandals (angels often are barefooted), carrying a water gourd, and with a backpack. Raphael is a friend to the traveler as well as others.

According to the Kabbalah, Raphael was one of the three angels that visited Abraham and Sarah. Another Jewish legend credits Raphael with giving Noah a "medical book" after the flood. It is postulated that this pharmaceutical tome may have been the famous *Sefer Raziel* (*The Book of the Angel Raziel*).

SEFER RAZIEL

The Book of Raziel is an ancient Kabbalah grimoire. The legend of the book is that it encompasses what the Angel Raziel revealed to Adam. It contains a large angelology, information on the planets in the solar system, protective spells, names of God, a method for writing healing amulets, and gematria, among other things.

Not only is Raphael a seraph, but he also belongs to three more celestial orders, including cherubim, dominions, and powers. As such an important archangel, Raphael has many high offices,

ARCHANGEL RAPHAEL WITH ADAM AND EVE

including regent of the sun, chief of the order of virtues, governor of the south and guardian of the west, ruling prince of the second heaven, overseer of the evening winds, and guardian of the Tree of Life in the Garden of Eden, to name some of the more impressive ones. He is also numbered among ten holy sefiroth of the Hebrew Kabbalah.

Uriel

In Jewish legend, Uriel ("flame of God") was the angel of hailstorms (presumably with lightning, since he is called fire), which would relate him to the Greek god Zeus, who had a habit of hurling thunderbolts of lightning when annoyed.

Moses encountered Uriel in the second heaven, and he is said to bring the light of the knowledge of God to humans. Milton named him a regent of the sun (along with Raphael) in *Paradise Lost*.

The soul at its highest is found like God, but an angel gives a closer idea of Him. That is all an angel is: an idea of God.

—MEISTER ECKHART

Uriel manifests as an eagle, and in the Book of Protection, he is described as a "spell-binding power" and is associated with Michael, Shamshiel, Seraphiel, and other powerful angels. The Zohar I says that Uriel governs the constellation of Virgo. He is said to be 300 parasangs tall and to be accompanied by a retinue of fifty myriads of angels. This entire multitude of attendant angels is made out of water and fire. It's not clear if some are water and some fire, or each a little of both, which seems a contradiction in terms—but, then, much of biblical lore and heavenly constructions is a contradiction in terms.

URIEL'S GRANDEUR

Uriel was indeed a grand form to behold. He was said to be 300 parasangs tall. A parasang is an ancient unit of measure that equates to about 3.5 miles. That means that Uriel stood about 1,050 miles tall! And Uriel was acoompanied by fifty myriads of angels. In Ancient Greek, a "myriad" was technically the number ten thousand, making Uriel's entourage 500,000 angels. Truly, this sight must have been something to behold.

Every visible thing in this world is put in the charge of an angel.

—ST. AUGUSTINE, *EIGHTY-THREE DIFFERENT QUESTIONS*

CHAPTER FIVE

The Hierarchy of the Angels

hy are angels arranged in hierarchies, a system of top-down organization, like the flowchart of corporate management? There are several reasons why various religions found this arrangement necessary. One was the sheer number of angels. The Jewish patriarchs produced angels swiftly and vigorously. The Catholic Church did its best to disband this trafficking in angels, but with little success, as it also named more and more angels. Even the great St. Augustine complained that angels "breed like flies."

A HOST OF ANGELS

AN ARMY OF ANGELS

There were so many angels that it made logical sense to get them in some kind of sequential order to manage the confusion about what kinds of angels did what tasks and which ones were closest to the throne of God. Since the Bible already had described angels as armies (which is what the word *host* means, as in "a host of angels"), the military scheme was employed, and the angels became arranged in ranks (in the same way that an army has generals, majors, captains, and lieutenants of various grades, and lower ranks from sergeant to buck privates. Mere angels, in this system, are privates.

CHERUBIM

Cherubim means "fullness of God's knowledge." It is related to the Assyrian word *karibu*, which means "one who prays" or "one who communicates." Cherubim continually praise god, never stopping or pausing.

In the Old Testament there were only two orders of angels, the seraphim and cherubim. Later, Dionysius the Areopagite, added seven more orders: Thrones, Dominions, Virtues, Powers, Principalities, Archangels, and Angels. St. Thomas Aquinas put his seal of approval on the matter in his many discourses on angels, and this was followed up in 1320 by Dante Alighieri, who in his *Divine Comedy* definitively ranked all creatures, the good and the bad.

The nine Celestial Orders and their ruling angels are as follows (angels may be part of multiple orders):

THE FIRST TRIAD (THE HIGHEST TRIAD)

- **Seraphim** are the highest order of angels. They surround the throne of God, ceaselessly singing his holy praises. They are the angels of love, light, and fire. Angels in the Seraphim include Michael, Seraphiel, Jehoel, Uriel, Kemuel, Metatron, Nathanael, and Satan (before his fall).

- **Cherubim** are the guardians of the fixed stars, keepers of the heavenly records, and bestowers of knowledge. They are the angels of harmony, protection, and wisdom and they channel positive energy from the divine. In the Talmud, cherubim are also related to the order of wheels, also called ophanim. Gabriel, Cherubiel, Ophaniel, Raphael, Uriel, Zophiel, and Satan (before his fall) are members of the Cherubim.

- **Thrones**, including the angels Orifiel, Zaphkiel, Zabkiel, Jolhiel (or Zophiel), and Raziel, are the angels who bring God's justice to earth. They are often called wheels or (in the Jewish Kabbalah) Chariots or the Merrabah.

THE SECOND TRIAD (MIDDLE TRIAD)

- **Dominions** are the divine leaders who regulate the angels' duties. They are the angels of intuition and wisdom, and the majesty of God is manifested through them. The Dominion angels are Zadkiel, Hashmal, Zacharael, and Muriel.

- **Virtues** are known as "the miracle angels." They are sent to earth to work miracles and are bestowers of grace and valor. These angels include Uzziel, Gabriel, Michael, Peliel, Barbiel, Sabriel, Haniel, Hamaliel, and Tarshish.
- **Powers** are the defenders and protectors of the world. They keep track of human history and they are the organizers of world religions. The Powers include Camael, Raphael, Verchiel, and Satan (before his fall).

THE THIRD TRIAD (LOWEST TRIAD)

- **Principalities**, including Nisroc, Naniel, Requel, Cerviel, and Amaelare, are the protectors of religion.
- **Archangels** rule over all the angels. The Archangels are Ariel, Azrael, Chamuel, Gabriel, Haniel, Jeremiel, Jophiel, Metatron, Michael, Raguel, Raphael, Raziel, Sandalphon, Uriel, and Zadkiel. Satan was also an archangel before his fall.
- **Angels** are the messengers of God working the closest with humanity. There are many different kinds of angels, including guardian angels. Their names are numerous and varied, but some include Phaleg, Adnachiel, Gabriel, and Chayyliel.

Scripture very rarely mentions angels, let alone hierarchical arrangements of them. Some modern religionists have taken issue with the very idea of angelic hierarchies. One, philosopher Mortimer Adler, finds such speculation "highly entertaining." And Christian writer Timothy Jones, in *Celebration of Angels*, states flatly:

Dionysius simply had no way to determine if his nine-fold ordering was literally true. Nor do we. Even Paul the apostle, who claimed to have been caught up into the "third heaven" (2 Corinthians 12:2), hinted that such things are not to be told. . . . Indeed, in Scripture, we gain only glimpses and fragments of how the angels might be organized. . . . However tantalizing the recorded glimpses of angels in Scripture are, they are ultimately just that: glimpses. We can take great comfort, however, in knowing that populating the heavenly spheres are creatures so great they boggle and frustrate our every attempt to pin them down.

FALLEN ANGELS

The war between God and the Fallen Angels, which can be interpreted as the conflict between good and evil, began when Lucifer—most beautiful and wise of all the beings created by the divine artificer and prince of the entire angelic order—decided to no longer bow to the authority of his sovereign Lord. In short, he rebelled against the highest authority.

It reads like the pilot plot for a new TV drama. Not only did the exquisitely beautiful and glamorously grand Lucifer decide to be entrepreneurial and go it on his own—like some rebellious VP who has been passed over for promotion—but rumor has it that he took at least a third of the angelic population along with him in the insurrection.

A FALLEN ANGEL

WHO ARE THE FALLEN ANGELS?

We don't know the names of all of the fallen angels, for there were a multitude of them—one-third of all the heavenly host—and they came from all the angelic ranks of principalities, virtues, cherubim, seraphim, and thrones. The poet John Milton listed those few who where named:

- Satan, the original Foul Fiend, a.k.a. the Devil himself
- Beelzebub, the second in command, a.k.a. the Lord of Flies
- Moloch, a nasty bit of business smeared with human blood
- Chemosh, a.k.a. Peor
- Baalim, a male spirit
- Ashtaroth, a female spirit
- Astoreth, another female spirit, who wore crescent horns (She is derived from Astarte, Queen of Heaven, a Phoenician goddess of fertility, beauty, and love, who corresponds to Babylonian Ishtar and Greek Aphrodite, all versions of the Great Mother Goddess. Note also that Hathor, the Egyptian mother goddess, wears crescent horns that represent the moon, and that all of these goddesses are Moon goddesses, emblematic of the feminine principle.)
- Azazel, a cherub of extraordinary height
- Mammon
- Thammuz
- Dagon
- Rimmon
- Belial, emblematic of lewdness

In Milton's version, all of these fallen angels lie together in Hell alongside the gods of the old pagan religions that predate the Bible—Egyptian Osiris and Isis and the entire Greek pantheon.

The name Lucifer became synonymous with Satan, also known as the Devil. In Hebrew, Satan means "adversary," and as a name, it was applied to the principle of evil, which was conceived by Judaism, Christianity, and Islam, as a person-like being. The word *devil* is derived from the Greek word for "accuser."

This fallen angel, by whatever name you choose, presides over Hell and is served by a coterie of minor angels, the ones who chose his side against God, and fell along with him to become devils (not with a capital *D* like "the Devil," a term reserved for Satan himself, once Prince of Light, now Prince of Darkness). The Devil has many other names as well: Abaddon, Apollyon, Dragon, Serpent, Asmodeus, Beelzebub or Baalzebub, and Belial.

Nowhere in Scripture are we told just *why* Lucifer/ Satan rebelled against God's authority. Ezekiel suggests that it was sheer vanity— pride in his own splendiferous gorgeous self, not to mention his possession of great wisdom.

GUARDIAN ANGELS

Guardian angels are among the angels in the lowest triad and they are the divine helpers closest to all living beings. Everyone has at least two guardian angels that will be with you from the time of birth to the time you pass from this earth plane. Your guardian angels are your personal angels and they are not assigned to anyone but you.

In whatever place you may be, in whatever secret recess you may hide, think of your Guardian Angel. . . . If we truly love our Guardian Angel, we cannot fail to have boundless confidence in his powerful intercession with God and firm faith in his willingness to help us. . . . Many of the saints made it a practice never to undertake anything without first seeking the advice of their Guardian Angel.

—ST. BERNARD OF CLAIRVAUX

GUARDIAN ANGEL

Your guardian angel is here to assist you in every aspect of your life and make your life easier if you let them. Your guardian angels love you with the same unconditional love as God, and there is nothing you could ever do or say that would change this love. Take time out of your busy schedule to pray with your guardian angels. Ask them for the help you need. Then listen, feel, and pay attention to how they answer your prayers. They know you very well and they know exactly how to get your attention.

ASCENDED MASTERS

Ascended masters are not mentioned in the hierarchy of angels, but they are God's divine helpers and they play their role in helping humanity evolve. During their lifetimes they were great teachers. These beings of light were once humans and they have now ascended into heaven. Their role is to help all those who need them.

HIERARCHY OF ASCENDED MASTERS

The ascended masters' place on the hierarchy is right below the archangels and above the angels. Just like the archangels, they have the ability to be with everyone simultaneously so they can serve all humans with great love and care.

Among these great beings and teachers are the Blessed Mother Mary, Jesus, Quan Yin, Buddha, Moses, Mohammed, Serapis Bey, Saint Theresa, and Saint Francis. The ascended masters have compassion and understanding of what you go through as a human being because they walked the journey themselves. They honor your free will and free choice, so you need to ask for their help. Trust that they will be by your side, instantaneously, ready to assist you in unconditional love. They are very powerful, enlightened beings and they have the ability to manifest healing and miracles into your life.

To people who live close to the earth, spirits live everywhere—in rocks and stones and trees and rivers and desert scrub. Divinity shines forth everywhere.

—SOPHY BURNHAM, *A BOOK OF ANGELS*

NATURE ANGELS

The fairies are sometimes called the angels of nature. Their vibration is very connected to the earth and their place in the hierarchy is in between the angels and humans. Fairies are very playful and creative and they love to hang around children. Because of this, children are more likely to see them, but they also like to assist adults, as well.

Fairies will nudge you to invite more play into your life, especially if your time is overloaded with work and family responsibilities. They love to play the role of matchmaker, and if you are looking for a soul mate they will help you find one. They love creativity and will provide inspiration to help you with any project: designing your gardens, your home, or any other creative endeavor. The fairies can play a powerful role in helping you manifest your dreams into reality.

LOVED ONES IN SPIRIT

Those who have died and transitioned into the spirit world resonate somewhere between the fairies and human beings. When you raise your vibration and connect your energy with the angelic realm, you will receive loving, supportive guidance that's directed from God. When you communicate with loved ones who have passed you may still be communicating with certain aspects of their personalities. For example, let's say that you want guidance from a particular relative in spirit about buying a new home. If he or she had been conservative in life and liked to save money, that personality trait would still be there. It might influence the guidance given.

ANGELS OF BIRTH AND DEATH

There are special "birth angels" who helped you enter this life experience, and there are also "death angels" that help you journey back home when it's time.

Many people believe that an infant is born with an "angel twin," the guardian angel that accompanies it throughout life. Others believe that there are special birth angels who attend the birth to make sure that all is well and then depart for other births. Other angels and spirits replace these earliest guardians as infants grow into childhood. The question of whether the first angel assigned to a child is its lifetime guardian angel has never been definitively answered.

A DEATH ANGEL

Angels also attend death. Emanuel Swedenborg, who wrote prolifically about angels, gives an account of how he first encountered "some of the kindest and most profoundly loving of all angels," in what we would today call a near-death experience. He explains that people "wake up" after dying, gradually becoming aware of angels at their heads. These "death angels" are apparently able to communicate with persons who have just died and make them feel peaceful, safe, and happily welcomed to their new state. The transition period, whether it is easy for the person that has passed or difficult (for some resist believing they are dead), is supervised by these special angels.

A host of angels flying,
Through cloudless skies impelled,
Upon the earth beheld
A pearl of beauty lying,
Worthy to glitter bright
In heaven's vast hall of light.

They saw, with glances tender,
An infant newly born,
O'er whom life's earliest morn
Just cast its opening splendor;
Virtue it could not know,
Nor vice, nor joy, nor woe.

The blest angelic legion,
Greeted its birth above,
And came, with looks of love,
From heaven's enchanting region;
Bending their wingèd way
To where the infant lay.

They spread their pinions o'er it,—
That little pearl which shone
With lustre all its own,—
And then on high they bore it,
Where glory has its birth;—
But left the shell on earth.

—DIRK SMITS, *ON THE DEATH OF AN INFANT*

... Six wings he wore, to shade

His lineaments Divine; the pair that clad

Each shoulder broad, came mantling
    o'er his brest

With regal Ornament; the middle pair

Girt like a Starrie Zone his waste, and
    round

Skirted his loines and thighes with
    downie Gold

And colors dipt in Hev'n; the third his
    feet

Shaddowd from either heele with
    featherd maile

Skie-tinctured grain.

—JOHN MILTON, *PARADISE LOST*

CHAPTER SIX

Angels in Art and Literature

ngels have a long tradition in art and literature.
However, depictions of them in stone are the first
forms of angel art we know. As history begins to
be recorded we find images of them in many cul-
tures around the world. These suggest that the notion of angels is
embedded in our psyches.

MILTON'S *PARADISE LOST*

In literature, the English poet John Milton (1608–74) gave the world the incomparable epic poems *Paradise Lost* and *Paradise Regained*, in which he undertook the daunting task of attempting to unravel the truth of the fallen angels and their impact on humanity. This is Milton's description of Raphael (from *Paradise Lost*):

> *Down thither prone in flight*
> *He speeds, and through the vast Ethereal Skie*
> *Sailes between worlds and worlds, with steddie wing*
> *Now on the polar windes, then with quick Fann*
> *Winnows the buxom air*

Milton built much of this epic poem around the unremitting heavenly warfare between the angels and their fallen brethren. Consider these lines:

> *The discord which befell, and War*
> *   in Heav'n*
> *Among th' Angelic Powers, and*
> *   the deep fall*
> *Of those too high aspiring, who*
> *   rebell'd*
> *With Satan.*

GOTHIC DESIGN

As Europe emerged from the Dark Ages and the great Gothic cathedrals began to rise during the twelfth through fifteenth centuries, the Gothic form dominated art and architecture. It was notable for its use of the high, pointed arch and ribbed vault with flying buttresses, which gave a flowing, soaring effect, the hallmark of Gothic architecture.

GOTHIC ARCH

Sculpture and stained glass windows were part of the Gothic design, and these magnificent cathedrals that seem to rise up into the very heavens were graced with beautiful depictions of the entire Christian story and included a plenitude of angels and angelic hosts. For example, the angels surrounding the main portal of the cathedral at Chartres, France, are there to express the sense of perfection of God's creation as well as the sense humans had developed of angels being their protectors and guides or guardians.

RUSSIAN AND GREEK ORTHODOX ICONS

In addition to Roman Catholicism, the Russian and Greek orthodox forms of Christianity contributed to great artistic renditions of angels (and saints). These brilliantly executed paintings, mostly on wood instead of canvas, are called icons. Their jewel-like mystical quality is riveting to the beholder's eye, and they are intended to be visual meditations for the purpose of direct contact with the image portrayed.

ANGELS IN ISLAMIC CULTURE

During the time of the Crusades, the concept of ideal beauty was beginning to be developed alongside the idealization of romantic love. This concept was popularized by the wandering troubadours during the twelfth century, especially in France. It was at this time that the great Sufi poet, Ibn Arabi, claimed that his major prose work, *The Meccan Revelations*, was dictated to him by the Angel of Inspiration. Another Sufi, Suhrawardi, left two major works, *The Crimson Archangel* and *The Rustling of Gabriel's Wing*, which are the richest documentation of angelic encounters in the Islamic culture.

GREEK ORTHODOX MADONNA ICON

REMBRANDT

In *Paradise Lost*, John Milton equates the archangel Gabriel with the chief of the angelic guards placed over Paradise. Gabriel is credited as the angel in the famous wrestling encounter with Jacob (though different sources credit Michael, Uriel, Metatron, Samael, and Chamuel with the role of the "dark antagonist"). No matter which angel was responsible for the fight, the famous scene was immortalized for all time in a canvas by Rembrandt.

MICHAEL

Michael, the Prince of the Heavenly Hosts, is always pictured in Renaissance paintings as young, strong, handsome, and wearing armor. He is supposed to be God's champion or chief warrior as well as the protector general of the Roman Catholic Church.

Michael is also known as the patron saint of the Hebrew nation, but the Jewish tradition forbids images or icons, so there's no Jewish religious art. The same is true of Islam, which forbids idolatry of images and which, therefore, has developed astonishingly beautiful geometric art forms to be viewed symbolically rather than literally.

Rembrandt was continually inspired to paint angels, many of which appear in his larger canvases; there are also glimpses of angels in his multitude of sketches. In these, the angels are more informal, charming, and approachable, especially the rendering of the archangel Raphael with Tobit, as companion on the journey.

DANTE'S *DIVINE COMEDY*

Dante Alighieri (1265–1321), in his *Celestial Hierarchies* compares God to a ray of cosmic light that, although it will always remain the "One," "becomes a manyness," dispersing itself and proceeding into the manifestation of the myriad universe and all in it from largest to tiniest.

This primal ray of light, according to Dante's interpretation of the angelic hierarchies, must be so arranged "that we might be led, each according to his capacity, from the most holy imagery to formless, unific, elevative principles and assimilations."

In Dante's concept, the angels, in a top-down manner, pass along God to humanity through all their ranks, from highest to lowest angels, until it reaches humans. You could say that every angelic appearance is in fact an appearance of God in disguise; rather like the Greek god Zeus, who appeared as a swan or a shower of gold because his full glory would incinerate the beholder. The Divine Light must be dimmed for human consumption.

Several centuries later, the French illustrator and painter Paul Gustave Doré (1832–83) would be inspired to create illustrations for Dante's *Divine Comedy*—magnificent, brooding etchings of demons

THE ANGEL DANTE CALLED "THE BIRD OF GOD"

writhing in the pits of hell and gloriously rendered angels—the entire heavenly host spiraling off into the infinite region of the most high.

In the *Divine Comedy* (*Purgatory*), Dante gives a vivid description of an angel at the helm of a boat, his wings flared upward, acting as sails, ferrying souls to their destination. Dante calls the angel "the Bird of God."

JOHN DONNE

Angels are represented equally well in both prose and poetry. The English poet John Donne (1572–1631) wrote of angels in his *Sermons on the Psalms and Gospels*: "I throw myself down in my Chamber and I . . . invite God and his angels thither, and when they are there, I neglect God and his angels for the noise of a fly, for the rattling of a coach, for the whining of a door."

Good night, sweet prince, and flights of angels sing thee to thy rest!

—WILLIAM SHAKESPEARE, *HAMLET*

In his *Devotions*, Donne says, "I consider thy plentiful goodness, O my God, in employing angels more than one, in so many of thy remarkable works." Detailing the many instances in Scripture in which not a single angel but a whole chorus (or crowd in the case of those ascending and descending Jacob's ladder) is seen, Donne continues: "From the first to their last, are angels, angels in the plural, in every service angels associated with angels."

WILLIAM BLAKE

At the time of his death, the English mystic-poet-engraver William Blake (1757–1827) was engaged in designing etchings to illustrate the *Divine Comedy*. Previously, Blake had executed and engraved many religious designs for his own lyrical poems. He wrote volumes about his experiences with angels and had great influence upon many of the major thinkers of his time. His legacy includes some of the most impassioned drawings of angels to ever come from the hand of an artist. Here is an excerpt from one of his texts:

> *It is not because angels are holier than men or devils that makes them angels, but because they do not expect holiness from one another, but from God only.*

THE PRE-RAPHAELITES

Blake was followed by a group of artists and writers who named themselves the Pre-Raphaelites. They formed a brotherhood of painters and poets in 1848 in protest against both the prevailing standards of British art and the oncoming rush of the Industrial Revolution, which threatened all handicrafts. They chose the name because their inspiration came from the work of Italian painters who predated Raphael (1483–1520). In ethereal tones, the Pre-Raphaelites depicted angels and angelic-like portraits of humans. But they were fated to fade away before the end of the nineteenth century, and with their passing, angels were eclipsed by the onset of technological "progress" and the new scientific materialism, neither of which needed them, pictorially or otherwise.

Yet, angels remained, carved in stone, etched on copper, painted on canvas; their images can be seen in nearly every city and town of the Western Hemisphere. They grace railway stations and libraries. They are seen on murals and friezes. They decorate war memorials and museum façades and are cast in bronze atop skyscrapers. They float gracefully on the domes of town halls. They are even seen on the walls of department stores, hospitals, and movie theaters. They stand in marble in the middle of park fountains or set upon pedestals in public squares. Wherever you look, you'll see an angel.

ARCHITECTURAL ANGELS

Softly and gently, dearly ransomed soul
In my most loving arms I now enfold thee,
And, o'er the penal waters, as they roll,
I poise thee, and I lower thee, and hold thee.
And carefully I dip thee in the lake,
And then, without a sob or a resistance,
Dost through the flood thy rapid passage take,
Sinking deep, deeper, into the dim distance.
Angels, to whom the willing task is given
Shall tend, and nurse, and lull thee, as thou liest;
And Masses on the earth, and prayers in heaven,
Shall aid thee at the throne of the Most Highest.
Farewell, but not for ever! brother dear,
Be brave and patient on thy bed of sorrow,
Swiftly shall pass thy night of trial here,
And I will come and wake thee on the morrow.

—JOHN HENRY NEWMAN, *THE DREAM OF GERONTIUS*

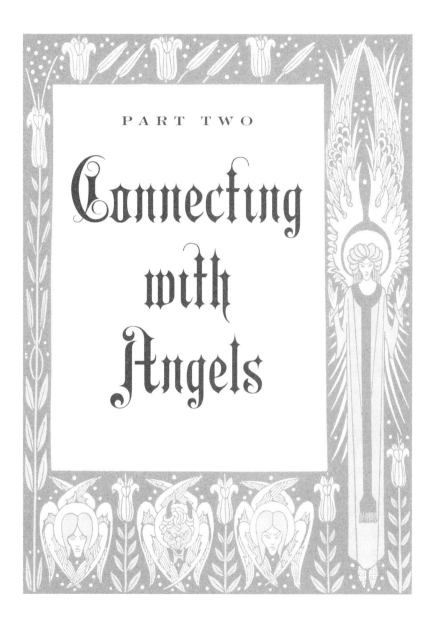

PART TWO

Connecting with Angels

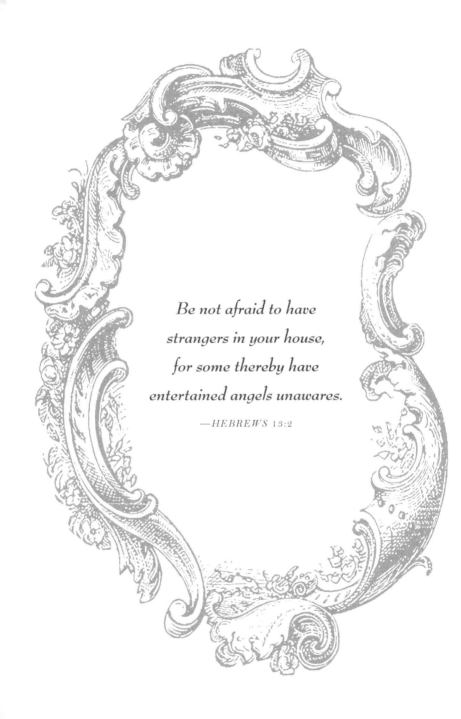

Be not afraid to have
strangers in your house,
for some thereby have
entertained angels unawares.

—*HEBREWS* 13:2

CHAPTER SEVEN

Raising Your Vibration

eaven and earth may seem like two different places, but they are one. To lift the veil and experience heaven you need to understand the concept of vibration. Think about a radio and how you can change the channel and tune into different stations to listen to various expressions of music. The same is true for the angelic realm. You simply need to attune your energy and raise your vibration to connect with the different hierarchies of angels.

ENERGY AND VIBRATION

You are energy and the angels are energy. If this is true, then why can't you see the angels like you can see other human beings? It has to do with the concept of vibration. One meaning of vibration from the *Merriam-Webster Dictionary* is, "a characteristic emanation, aura, or spirit that infuses or vitalizes someone or something and that can be instinctively sensed or experienced." Here is the key: In order to see or feel the energy of the angels, you need to raise your vibration to be in tune with their energy. The angels vibrate in the energy of pure divine love and humans resonate between the energy of fear and love.

CHANGE YOUR MOOD WITH A SMILE

If you're ever having a bad day and want to feel better, simply smile. Fake it if you need to. Try it right now; smile and see how you feel. Notice how your energy changes. This is a simple technique to raise your vibration. You can change any situation, no matter where you are or who you are with, by just smiling.

The energy of fear resonates at a lower vibration, while the energy of love resonates at a higher vibration. Think about the last time you were around someone who was angry, depressed, or confused. What "vibe" did you get from that person? Did he lift you up or bring you down? Now think of an occasion when you were with someone who was fun and who made you laugh. What vibe did you get from this person? Did her energy lift your spirits or bring you down?

If you would like to hear, feel, and see the angels, you need to raise your vibration to become one with their energy. There are different ways of doing this. Try one or two of the following methods to see which one works best for you.

LISTEN TO YOUR WORLD

In order to experience the presence of angels, you must turn off the electronic sounds around you. In order to come to your spiritual center, listen to the simpler sounds around you. You might hear a bird chirping, rain dripping, or the simple sound of your own breath.

SILENCE

When you sit in stillness and silence, your mind and body relax. By becoming still, you can find your center, where the ego mind quiets and the gateway to the divine opens. The angels want to get your attention and communicate with you, and it's easier when you can find this place to connect.

Around our pillows, golden ladders rise,
And up and down the skies,
With winged sandals shod,
The angels come and go, the messengers of God!

—R.H. STODDARD, *HYMN TO THE BEAUTIFUL*

Silence is the pathway to follow on your journey to the center of the self. In silence, you begin to experience a unity and recognize you are one with the divine. Almost everyone has had this experience at some time, perhaps while sitting by a lake in silence and solitude, gazing at a sleeping child, or caught alone and awestruck by a magnificent sunset on a country road. These are mystical moments that connect you to the larger world of which you are a part. You are transfixed and transformed for the moment. This feeling happens in the silence, and this is where you can sense, feel, and experience the angels.

When we listen, we hear our angel voices in the shadows and the light places of peace and darkness within us. . . . The voices of our angels bear witness to the triumphs of Spirit.

—KAREN GOLDMAN, *ANGEL VOICES*

In the silence of the inner self, you reach truth, and in so doing, you find your angels, guiding and gracing you and delivering the messages you need to hear. The angels want to help you and they want you to be able to recognize their presence in your life.

Fortunately, you do not have to retire to a monastery or become a hermit to experience the contemplative silence that is at the heart of experiencing the angelic world. You can achieve your own silence and recognize the presence of angels by practicing silence on a daily basis.

GUIDED MEDITATION

If you have a difficult time sitting in silence because your mind is too busy, you might want to try guided meditation. Most guided meditations combine soothing music with the use of visualization. Both techniques help you relax and to enhance the experience. You can sit back and relax as you are soothed by the music, and all you need to do is follow the guide's voice as it brings you into meditation. Your thoughts are focused on following the direction of the guide and it's easier to let go as you allow your experiences to unfold.

Make yourself familiar with the angels, and behold them frequently in spirit; for, without being seen, they are present with you.

—ST. FRANCIS DE SALES

Most guided meditations start with a deep relaxation of the body and the mind. After you slow down your breath and release the tension in your body, you will physically and mentally relax. When this happens you naturally open up the pathway to other states of consciousness. In these altered states you can enhance your spiritual growth and development and you can communicate with the angels.

The following guided meditation will help you raise your vibration so you can attune to the angels and receive their guidance. During this attunement you can release your fears and ask the angels for the help you need. They will help you raise your vibration so you can feel them, hear them, and possibly see them.

It will be helpful if you record the words beforehand so you can simply relax and listen during the meditation. Remember to speak slowly and with a soothing voice when you record the meditation. Try playing soothing music in the background during your recording.

GUIDED MEDITATION FOR
RAISING VIBRATION

Take some deep breaths and close your eyes. Set the intention with your angels to attune to their energy and raise your vibration so you can easily see, feel, hear, and sense their loving presence. (Pause)

Ask the angels to surround you in a beautiful circle of divine light, love, and protection. Take a moment and breathe with them and feel their unconditional love flow into every cell of your being. As you do this, your body begins to relax. Feel this soothing and healing divine light flow into the top of your head, relaxing your scalp; all the muscles in your scalp relax. Now, feel it flow into your forehead and then your eyes, cheeks, jaw, and your mouth. All the muscles in your face relax. (Pause) Feel the light and relaxation flow into your neck, relaxing your neck. Feel it flow into your shoulders, down your arms, and to the tips of your fingers. It feels so good to relax and let go. (Pause) Breathe the divine light into your chest and feel all your muscles relax in your chest. Then feel it flow into your stomach and all the muscles in your stomach relax. (Pause) Now, bring awareness to your back, and feel the divine light flow down your back relaxing your upper back, your middle back, all the way down to your lower back. Your entire back relaxes in this beautiful soothing light. (Pause) Feel as the light and relaxation flow down into your hips, your knees, your calves, and all the way down to the soles of your feet, the tips of your toes. (Pause) Your entire body is filled with relaxation and the divine light. Every cell of your being is illuminated with this divine light. Notice how good it feels to relax and let go. (Pause)

Imagine the angels give you a beautiful cloud chair and they ask you to sit in it and relax. This chair was made just for you and it fits you perfectly. You melt into the cloud chair and relax even deeper. (Pause) Feel and imagine 10,000 angels surrounding you. Welcome them, breathe with them, and know they are there to help you. (Pause) Imagine your cloud chair being carried upward into the higher vibration of the angelic realm where only love exists. They know exactly what they are doing, so just trust and allow them to attune your energy to this higher vibration of love and light. (Pause) As you relax, notice what you feel, what you hear, what you see, and what you sense. (Pause) Take a moment and release your fears to the angels. They have the ability to dissolve them so you can receive healing and clarity. (Pause) Now, share with them your prayers and desires. Ask for the help you need. (Pause) Trust that your prayers have been heard and that they will be answered.

This attunement has transformed you. From this moment forward, you will be more in tune with the angels that surround you. You will sense their energy around you. You will hear more clearly their messages of divine guidance. You will understand how they are trying to get your attention. Because of this attunement, you will experience more joy, peace, fulfillment, and happiness in your life. You deserve it and the angels are there to help you create it. Just remember to ask for their help when you need it. You are never, ever alone, and you are loved unconditionally by God and the angels.

Take a moment to thank the angels. (Pause) Ask that they continue to guide you in every way.

Now feel or imagine the angels bringing your cloud chair slowly back into the present moment. Take some deep breaths and feel as you ground yourself in the moment of now. Feel light, free, and grateful, and filled with light and love. (Pause) Expect peace. Expect miracles. Expect better than you could ever imagine.

Use this guided meditation whenever you want to relax or if you want to ask the angels for help and guidance. They are always there for you, and guided meditation can be a powerful tool to help you make that connection.

WORKING WITH THE BREATH

Angels are pure spirit, and you can raise your vibration and enhance your connection to their world simply by using breath techniques. By becoming aware of your breathing, you become aware of your spiritual nature, for breath is life. Thus, you can use your breath, as a yogi does, to elevate your consciousness to the realm where the angels dwell. In other words, the breath is the gateway to the sacred angelic dimension.

Breath is something you take for granted. Without breath there is no life. Most times you are unaware of your breathing until you experience a shortness of breath or panic sets in and your breath speeds up. When you become aware of your breathing you connect to your spiritual self. Awareness and control of breath allow you to consciously raise your vibration and connect to the sacred realm.

When you enhance the breath and use it to open up to different realms, your natural abilities begin to unfold—mental, physical, emotional, and spiritual. It unblocks energy and channels of communication open up; information can flow into your consciousness. Conscious breathing develops a communications link between body and mind, between conscious and unconscious, between spirit and angels.

Here is a rhythmic breathing technique that you can use at any time to raise your vibration. You can do it almost anywhere, whether sitting quietly at home, in your car, or when walking. It's simple and it can help you connect with your inner power.

RHYTHMIC BREATHING TECHNIQUE

Relax and close your eyes. Observe your breath pattern, but do not make any attempt to alter it. Just pay attention to the breath going in and coming out. Now, begin to breathe slowly and deeply. Feel the warmth of used air leave your body and breathe in fresh clean air. Imagine yourself being cleansed and energized by each breath.

Now listen to the sounds you make while you're breathing. Notice whether you breathe in shallow or deep breaths and where the air goes—into the diaphragm or the belly. Does your chest rise or fall or does your abdomen rise or fall?

As you inhale and exhale, allow the breath to become one continuous movement (with no separation or gaps between the inhale and the exhale). Continue doing this for several minutes and notice how you feel.

AFFIRMATIONS

You can empower yourself by changing your thoughts from the negative to the positive. You can do this by writing or saying an affirmation. An affirmation is a truth declared through a positive statement. For example, if you are continuously saying, "There must not be angels because I cannot see or feel them," change that statement and affirm, "I know there are plenty of angels here for me. I am willing to see and feel their loving presence." An affirmation helps you to raise your vibration to experience the possibilities of the angelic realm. If your thoughts are filled with fear and doubt you will continue to experience the same. Sometimes, you'll need to fake it until you make it through the use and power of affirmations. When you practice using affirmations, you shift your thoughts to experience what you want versus what you don't want. It creates a power that opens the gateways to experience miracles.

CHANTING

Chanting is an ancient ritual, and it's been used in different religious and ritual ceremonies to access the divine. Through the power of chanting you can reach altered states of consciousness and raise your vibration to connect with the divine. Chanting can transform negative energy into positive energy, which immediately raises your vibration. When you chant certain phrases over and over again, it shifts the vibration and causes change in mind, body, and spirit. You quiet the mind, you open the heart, and you lift your spirit to a higher state of consciousness.

There are no hard-set rules for chanting. You can chant anywhere—in the shower, at work, in the car, or while you're walking outdoors.

Here are some different forms of chanting you can practice.

- The OM chant is a universally recognized chant. Take in a breath, then on the out breath draw out the sound of OM like this: "oooooommmmmmmmmmmm," putting the emphasis on the last part.
- Gregorian chant is a beautiful form of music and chanting. You can buy Gregorian chant recordings online. Play them during meditation or listen to them in the car. You can also seek out a local church that sings this medieval form of music.
- Use a mala, a string of beads used to count mantras or Sanskrit prayers. A mantra can be a word or series of words chanted out loud. As you touch each bead, repeat your mantra. You can use a Sanskrit mantra meaning peace— "Shanti, Shanti, Shanti"—or you can repeat English words like "I am" or "love."
- Use rosary beads and say one of the following prayers: Our Father, Hail Mary, or Glory Be.

Experiment and see what form of chanting creates a connection between you and the divine. When you make that connection, you will feel it in every cell of your being.

SURROUND YOURSELF WITH POSITIVE PEOPLE

Reflect for a moment on how you feel when you are surrounded by people who are positive, encouraging, and uplifting. You may feel lighter, happier, or even empowered. If the opposite is true and there is negativity around you, you possibly feel drained, frustrated, and unmotivated.

To raise your vibration, seek out like-minded people who are interested in spirituality and the angels. You will learn from each other and together you will expand your awareness.

Release Fear and Remember Love

Fear can clog your energy centers or chakras. It lowers your vibration and blocks the flow of divine guidance. It's important to become conscious of when you are focusing on fear. Choose to recognize it, stop it, and focus on the positive. Fear comes in many forms: worry, stress, confusion, anger; the list goes on. Feel the low vibration of these energies and imagine how it can weigh you down. In each and every moment, you can make a choice to let go of fear and focus your thoughts on faith. Ask the angels to lift your fears and help you remember your choices based on love.

The angels vibrate in the energy of pure love. So as you work to clear your blocks of fear and replace them with love, faith, and trust, you naturally raise your vibration to experience the angels. You can hear their loving guidance. You can see them in their loving presence and you can sense them all around you. Isn't it worth taking the time to change your thoughts from fear to love?

No, I never saw an angel, but it is irrelevant

whether I saw one or not. I feel their

presence around me.

—PAULO COELHO

Gratitude

Gratitude is a wonderful way to open up the energy of your heart chakra. Each and every time you have thoughts of gratitude or you recognize the blessing in your heart, you raise your vibration and heighten your awareness of the miracles all around you.

KEEP A JOURNAL

Start your day or end your day by writing ten things you are grateful for. It is so simple and it can transform your life. If you choose, you can multiply the blessings in your life and open your awareness to experience the graces of the angels all around you.

Practice recognizing the small things in life you are grateful for: a thank you or a smile from a stranger, a good cup of coffee, a sunny day, or finding time to read a good book. To raise your vibration during difficult times, choose to focus on the blessings in your life. For example, if you are going through financial difficulties, be grateful for having the money to pay the essentials, food and shelter. If you are challenged with a physical illness, be grateful for those who are there to help you in your time of need. If you are grieving a loss or separation from a family member or close friend, focus on the love and support of those that are still in your life. You have the power and the choice to change any situation in your life. Choose to start today and focus on the positive, focus on the love in your life, and expect life to change for the better.

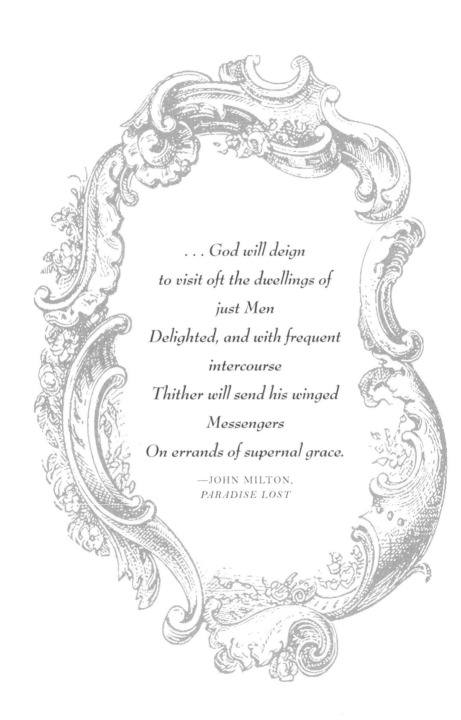

. . . God will deign
to visit oft the dwellings of
just Men
Delighted, and with frequent
intercourse
Thither will send his winged
Messengers
On errands of supernal grace.

—JOHN MILTON,
PARADISE LOST

CHAPTER EIGHT

Communicating with the Angels

he foundation is laid and it's time to start your communication with your angels. The angels are just as excited to connect with you, and it is an honor for them to serve you and guide you along your journey. Be open and experiment with the different suggestions. Discover what feels right for you and which method provides you with a direct link to experience heaven on earth.

CREATING A SACRED SPACE

Your sacred space is a place of retreat where you can step away from your busy everyday life. It's a quiet, peaceful place where you can connect with the loving presence and assistance of the angels. You don't need to wait until you have a whole room available. A favorite chair, a small corner of your home or apartment, a bench outdoors, or even the shower can be a perfect place to retreat where no one can bother you.

ASK FOR BLESSINGS

A wonderful way to start your day is to enter your sacred space and ask the angels to fill your day with blessings. Ask them to show you what you need to know throughout the day. Enter again at night and release your worries and fears to the angels. Complete your day with gratitude and thank the angels for all that they do.

Picture your sacred space as a little getaway where you can experience safety, peace, and clarity. Here are some suggestions for creating your sacred space:

- Play peaceful music.
- Display pictures of your favorite religious deities.
- Display pictures of your loved ones living or deceased.
- Light candles to create the energy.
- Place crystals or rocks collected from meaningful places.

- Place pictures or statues of angels.
- Find a special journal to write in.
- Have a fountain with the soothing sound of water.
- Turn off your phone.

Your sacred space is where you can let go, pray, and be open to the gifts and miracles of the angels. Each time you enter your space, invite the angels to gather and ask them to surround you in their loving light and protection. Ask them to fill your space with the highest vibration of divine white light and energy, and know that with each breath you take, you will become one with this sacred healing light.

MEDITATION

Meditation is one of the most powerful ways to connect and communicate with the angelic realm. Your body relaxes and the chatter in your mind slows down so you can connect with the higher vibration of the angels that surround you. The sensations in your body are more attuned to feel the love and warmth of the angels. Your mind quiets and the pathways open so you can hear messages of divine guidance. Meditation will also create a space where it's easier for the angels to communicate with you because the outside distractions of the world are silenced.

Make a point to schedule some quality time for meditation. You can start with ten minutes. Spend some time in prayer and share with the angels your concerns and requests. As you discover the benefits from taking this time for yourself, you might want to experiment with listening to a guided meditation recording or spend some time writing your thoughts to the angels.

Some people benefit from the group energy in a meditation class or retreat. It may help you to connect with other like-minded people and a facilitator who can give you some guidance and answer your questions. Trust and know that there is no right or wrong way to meditate; it's a matter of experimenting and discovering the best method for you.

Angels and angelic spirits serve us in many other ways during our life before death. When we need more strength or courage or clearer direction than we feel we have within ourselves, our appeals for help . . . bring angelic assistance if those appeals are genuine and if we are willing to accept help. . . . Most frequently, the support or guidance comes through spiritual depths that lie beneath our consciousness: when we become aware of them the strength or direction seems to have come from within—from some previously unknown resource.

—ROBERT H. KIRVEN, *ANGELS IN ACTION*

MEETING YOUR GUARDIAN ANGEL

Can you imagine what it would feel like to know that you are never alone and you have an angel watching over you and protecting you at all times? God assigned you at least two guardian angels at the time of your birth and they will be with you until the time that you leave this earth plane. Remember, you have to ask your guardian angels to be a part of your life.

We cannot pass our guardian angel's bounds,
resigned or sullen, he will hear our sighs.

—SAINT AUGUSTINE

There are different ways to connect with your guardian angels. First, share your desires with them. If you want to meet them in your meditation or dream state, ask them to make their presence known to you. If you want to feel comforted by their love or you want to know that you are safe and protected, ask your guardian angels to help you feel this. If you want to receive messages of guidance, ask them to help you hear their loving voices through your thoughts.

MEDITATION TO CONNECT WITH
YOUR GUARDIAN ANGEL

Get comfortable and close your eyes and take a couple of deep breaths. (Pause) Let go of whatever happened before your meditation and do the same for whatever is going to take place after your meditation. This is your special time and you are going to meet your guardian angel. Imagine yourself in a beautiful meadow: the sun's shining, it's a beautiful day, and nature is singing all around you. The beautiful soothing light from the sun relaxes you and comforts you. (Pause)

As you look ahead, you see a beautiful path and you go toward the path, intrigued by where it may lead. As you follow the path you feel lighter and lighter. (Pause) It leads you into the most beautiful garden you have ever seen. This is your soul's garden. You can see, feel, and create all the beauty you desire in your garden. If you want waterfalls, there are waterfalls. If you desire animals, beautiful flowers, and colors, it's all there. Create the garden of your wishes. Know that it's peaceful, it's sacred, and there is so much love in this garden. (Pause) Now, look for that perfect place to sit and rest. It could be a bench, a hammock, or you may just lie on the ground. (Pause) Know that as you sit in this beautiful place, your desire is to meet your guardian angel. Call out and ask your guardian angel to come close so you can feel or see her presence and know beyond any doubt that this is your guardian angel. Sit in silence, breathe, and receive. (Pause) When you're ready, ask your guardian angel if she has a message for you. (Pause) Ask that your guardian angel continue to guide you to the answers to your prayers. Share if there is anything you need help with. Thank your guardian angel and express your desire that you would like your guardian angel to continue to make her presence known to you.

Your guardian angels' mission is to serve and guide you. If you allow them, they can be your best friends, your teachers, and your bodyguards in spirit.

WRITING WITH YOUR ANGELS

Journaling with your angels can be both healing and enlightening. Some people do very well with this technique of communication. Writing the messages might make it easier for you to bypass your intellectual mind so you can allow the pen to record the angelic thoughts flowing through your consciousness.

One way to start is to clear your mind. You can do this by writing on paper all the thoughts that go through your mind. They can be mundane like, "I loved my cup of coffee this morning" or they can be filled with stress and fear like, "I don't know how I am going to pay my mortgage this month." Just write and fill the pages until the pen stops or your mind quiets.

START YOUR DAY WITH ANGELS

Try writing with your angels early in the morning before you start your day. The mind is clearer, and what a beautiful way to start the day, with a message from your angels.

After your mind is clear, turn to a blank page and write at the top of the page, "My dearest angels, what would you like to say to me today?" Then breathe in the love of the angels all around you; listen, feel, and write down whatever comes to you. If you get images or colors, write them down. If you just get words, write them down. If you receive feelings, record the feeling. Trust that as you put your pen to the paper and you start writing, the words will come. Try not to think about what you are writing and certainly don't concern yourself with spelling; just write and let it flow. The more you practice, the easier it gets and the more the words just flow onto the paper.

Asking a Specific Question

You can use writing to ask your angels to answer a specific question. Again, clear your mind through meditation or release your thoughts by writing them on paper. Then ask your angels to guide you during your writing session and ask them to lead you to your highest and best. On a blank piece of paper, write at the top, "Dearest angels, please give me your guidance on the following question (then write your question)." Breathe with the angels; listen, feel, and write down anything that comes to you. When you read your message, notice how it feels. If it is loving, encouraging, and supportive then this is a message from your angels. Then ask for guidance, ask for peace, and allow yourself to receive the answers you are searching for. Trust that these messages can flow easily through the clarity of your thoughts onto the paper.

Angel Mail

This is a very powerful yet playful way to communicate with your angels. The angels want you to surrender your worries and prayers to them so they can help you. When you hold on so tight to your issues or when you want to control the outcome of your life, you get in your own way and it's harder for the angels to help you. Sending angel mail is a wonderful way to let go and ask for help. Write a letter to your angels and share your prayers, worries, and concerns, both for yourself and others. Then put it in an envelope and symbolically or literally mail it to God and the angels. As you mail it, surrender it and trust that it will be read and heard. Ask for divine resolution to occur and then let it go.

This is a wonderful technique for children to use. They can color or write their prayers or fears on paper and together you can mail it to the angels. After you share this gift with your child, watch the peace on her face as she puts the letter in the mailbox.

SPEND TIME IN NATURE

In nature you can let go of the outside world and you can take time to breathe. You can distance yourself from the distractions that clog your mind and your emotions. Nature can be a very healing place if you allow yourself to receive its gifts.

Millions of spiritual creatures walk the earth—unseen, both when we wake and when we sleep.

—JOHN MILTON, *PARADISE LOST*

No matter what time of year it is, you can commune with the angels and the energy of God in nature. Leave your headphones at home and walk in silence, listen, and breathe. Ask the angels to

clear your energy and your mind. Imagine the wind taking away all your cares and worries. Ask for guidance, ask for peace, and allow yourself to receive the answers you are searching for. The message might come from the sounds of nature or through the clarity of your thoughts.

TALKING TO YOUR ANGELS IN THE CAR

God and the angels are everywhere and they are even present while you are driving in your car. So make the car your sacred space. Turn off the radio and invite your angels into your car. Ask your guardian angel to sit in the passenger seat and ask your other angels to fill the back seat. Then breathe with the comfort and support of knowing they are there with you. The angels are great listeners, so share with them your worries, fears, and concerns. Ask for the help you need so you can experience peace, balance, and joy.

It sounds so simple, but this time can be precious for those on the go. You will find that spending this time in silence and communion with your angels will create blessings throughout your entire day.

DREAM WITH THE ANGELS

Dream encounters with the angels have been described both in the Bible and in other sacred texts. Their visitations are also experienced by the everyday person. The average person spends eight hours a day sleeping, so this time can be used very wisely when working with the angels.

When you're sleeping, your conscious mind steps back, and because of this, you can get out of your own way and open up to other realms of consciousness. Before you go to sleep at night, ask the angels to enter your dream state. You can ask for help with the following in your dream state:

- Ask the angels for any healing you need—physical, emotional, or mental.
- Ask the angels to help you connect with your loved ones in spirit so you can receive a message that they are okay.
- Ask the angels for guidance about anything in your life.
- Ask the angels for spiritual teaching or help in learning what you need to know to further your development.
- Ask the angels to help you travel to other places and other times.
- Ask the angels to help you connect with them and any other guides or divine helpers that want to work with you.

Before you go to bed, make this affirmation: "Dearest angels, please enter my dreamtime tonight and help me with healing and share with me your clear messages of divine guidance. Please help me remember whatever I need to know when I awaken. Thank you." Keep a dream journal by your bed and when you wake up, record all your thoughts and impressions from the night before. You may be able to interpret some dreams immediately, while other dreams may be more symbolic and you might not understand them in that moment. Continue to record your dreams and, in time, your symbolism will transform into meaningful insight.

All God's angels come
to us disguised.

—JAMES RUSSELL LOWELL

As you can see, there are many fun and different ways to explore and experiment with as you learn to communicate and connect with your angels. Play with them and enjoy each one. Discover which methods work best for you and continue your practice as you create a beautiful relationship and channel of communication between yourself and the angels.

For He will command His angels concerning you to guard you in all your ways; they will lift you up in their hands, so that you will not strike your foot against a stone.

—*PSALM* 91:11–12

CHAPTER NINE

Protection from the Angels

veryone wants to feel safe and protected, especially in a world where bad things happen and life can be unpredictable. The angels want you to feel safe because fear can immobilize you. It can hold you back from living your life to the fullest. Open your heart and ask for protection for you and your loved ones, and learn how you can move into the unknown with more peace, trust, and adventure.

FEAR VERSUS FAITH

Fear is a strong emotion that you experience when you feel in danger or you anticipate that something bad might happen. Fear triggers a feeling of being out of control, and your greatest fear becomes the fear of the unknown. The mind starts imagining scenarios that might take place and your subconscious mind replays all the tapes from your past memories that are associated with fear. These memories could be your personal experiences, a friend or family member's experience, or something you witnessed through the media. No matter the source, the fearful memory creates an emotion that causes unnecessary stress, anxiety, and worry.

Here are some examples of fear:

- **You are listening to the news and you hear a child has been abducted.** You immediately go into fear about your own child. Your thoughts might be, "Should I pick him up at school today?" or "It's not safe, so he can't go outside and play."
- **You're on a plane, leaving for vacation.** Your thoughts are focused on the house: "Did I leave the stove on? What if there's a fire?" or "What if someone knows we're not home?"
- **Your daughter is at college.** Your thoughts are focused on fear and not on trusting your daughter: "What if she walks home alone in the dark?" or "What if she is influenced by others and gets involved in drugs or drinking?"

Take a moment and notice how you feel reading these scenarios and then reflect back to your own personal experiences and recognize when you've allowed yourself to be carried away by your fearful thoughts.

Whenever this happens it's time to call on the angels for protection and ask them to help you transform your fear into faith. As you do this, you will feel yourself released from the grip of fear, and in that moment you can take back your power and choose more peaceful and empowering thoughts.

Here are different ways to react to the same examples:

- **You are listening to the news and you hear a child has been abducted.** You say a prayer for the child and her family. Then you ask 10,000 angels to surround your children in divine light and protection.
- **You're on a plane, leaving for vacation.** You ask the angels to watch over your house and your valuables while you're gone.
- **Your daughter is at college.** You call on Archangel Michael and your daughter's guardian angels and ask them to watch over her and you affirm, "Only good can come to her. She is smart and she makes good decisions."

Notice the difference between the two sets of examples. Ask yourself which feels better and which one you would choose to practice. The angels want to help you transform your fear into faith. They know that it will not only help you, but it will help the lives of everyone else around you.

Exercise to Transform Fear Into Faith

This is an exercise you can use when you experience fear of any kind. The first step is to recognize that you are having a physical response that's connected to the fearful thoughts that are running through your mind. You might be thinking, "What if…" and all your thoughts are focused on the bad things that could happen or the harmful circumstances that might occur. Next, get grounded in the present moment by taking a deep breath and acknowledging that you're afraid. Call on the Archangel Michael and as many angels as you want. Ask for help. Tell them you're afraid and you want to feel safe, protected, and calm. Then just breathe with them, imagining that they are surrounding you in a protective shield of light where no harm can come to you. Remind yourself of where you are and affirm to yourself, "I am in the present moment and the angels are surrounding me and protecting me in their loving light. Please, angels, release me from this fear and help me feel the presence of God's love." Continue breathing deeply until the physical reactions in your body subside. Focus your thoughts on the angels and the word "faith." When you feel more peaceful, continue to imagine yourself in the protective divine light, knowing that you are encircled by heavenly helpers.

ANGELS OF PROTECTION

Some angels and archangels have a specific role: to watch over and protect humanity. As you read about each angel, pay attention to your feelings and notice which angels you feel connected to. Then call them by name and ask for the help you need. Trust that they will immediately assist you and that they will be at your side in comfort and protection.

Archangel Michael Provides Protection

Archangel Michael is the leader of the archangels. He is the archangel of protection and the patron saint of policemen. He carries a sword that symbolizes his ability to cut through all fear and resistance. He lends his courage and his strength to anyone who calls on him. Michael has a fiery energy, and when you invoke him it's very possible you might feel warm or even begin to sweat. You might see the colors purple and blue, which are associated with Archangel Michael's

presence. Call on Archangel Michael, and he will help you with protection of all kinds. He will empower you with the courage you need for any situation.

PRAYER TO ARCHANGEL MICHAEL

Archangel Michael, please come to me now and surround me in your protective shield of light. Please clear my energy field and release me from all negativity. Help me feel safe and protected in your loving presence and provide me with the courage I need.

Archangel Raphael Protects Travelers

Archangel Raphael is not only a healer, but he protects travelers of all kinds. Call on Raphael when you want to feel safe and protected while traveling. Ask that your journey, from beginning to end, be experienced with ease and protection.

PRAYER TO ARCHANGEL RAPHAEL

Archangel Raphael, I know you are with us at all times. I ask for your assistance during our travels. Please protect me and all concerned so we feel surrounded in God's loving presence until we reach our destination safely and with ease.

Archangel Ariel Protects the Environment and Animals

Archangel Ariel's name means "lion or lioness of God." She is committed to helping heal and protect Mother Nature, which includes all animals. She is the protector of the waters. She watches over all bodies of water and aquatic life. Ariel also protects those who travel upon the water, like fishermen. If you feel concerned about the environment and you want to do your part in protecting it, call on Ariel for support and help.

When your pets are sick or in trouble, ask both Archangel Ariel and Archangel Raphael to intervene. Ask them to watch over your pets and trust that they will receive the protection and healing they need.

PRAYER TO ARCHANGEL ARIEL TO PROTECT MOTHER NATURE

Archangel Ariel, I see that Mother Nature needs some healing and balance. Please watch over all of her inhabitants and see that they are protected from all harm. Please bring healing to the earth and remind me how I can play my part in helping and healing Mother Nature.

PRAYER TO ARCHANGEL ARIEL AND ARCHANGEL RAPHAEL FOR YOUR PETS

Archangel Ariel and Archangel Raphael, please watch over _____. Surround her in your healing and protective divine light. Comfort her and remind her she is not alone and she is loved. Help her to heal completely and feel healthy, whole, and vibrant once again. Thank you, Ariel and Raphael; with you taking care of her I trust that all is well.

Archangel Zaphiel Protects Children

Archangel Zaphiel is the leader of the choir of cherubim. He watches over children and will help them in any way he can. If they are having trouble in school, with friends, at home, or even with physical or emotional issues, ask Zaphiel to watch over and protect them. Imagine him wrapping his wings around them and protecting them in love.

PRAYER TO ARCHANGEL ZAPHIEL

Archangel Zaphiel, I know God loves my children dearly. Please help_____ and bring divine resolution to the following situation _____. Please wrap them in your wings of love and protection and help them feel safe and loved in your divine presence. I trust that they will receive exactly what He needs for His highest and best, better than I could ever imagine.

Suriel Protects Your Home and Possessions

Suriel is named in the Kabbalah as the angel who rules over the earth. He will watch over your home and possessions. Whenever you recognize that you're focused on fear, call on Suriel and ask him to keep your home and your possessions safe.

PRAYER TO ARCHANGEL SURIEL

Archangel Suriel, please watch over our home and our possessions at all times. Surround our home with angels and keep it safe and protected. Fill it with love and light so only good can come into our home.

Laylah Protects Newborns

Laylah is an angel of the night, and his name comes from the Hebrew word meaning sleep. Laylah watches over infants and helps them move through the adjustment of being in a physical body. If you are a mother with a newborn child, call on Laylah for help. Ask him to watch over your precious child with love, compassion, and protection.

PRAYER TO LAYLAH

Please watch over my newborn _____. Help him adjust beautifully and easily into his new life. Let him know how dearly loved he is and that we are happy he is here and that he chose us as parents. Keep him safe and protected and help me feel calm and peaceful as I adjust to being a new mother.

These angels and archangels of protection are honored to assist you along your journey. They know how vulnerable you feel when fear takes over. Call them by name and know that their role is to protect you and shield you from all harm.

PROTECTING YOURSELF FROM NEGATIVITY

Negative situations or people can drain your energy. When you're around someone who is very controlling or even needy, that person can deplete your energy supply, leaving you feeling drained and exhausted. The same feeling may occur when you have to partici- pate in high-pressure situations or you have to visit someone who is going through a very stressful time. It's important to recognize these situations when they arise and call on the angels of protec- tion for help. The following are situations where you can call on the angels of protection:

- When visiting a hospital or someone who is ill
- When attending a funeral
- When you have to go to court for any reason
- When there is a lot of negativity in your work place
- When dealing with authoritative figures
- When you need to do any kind of public speaking
- When you work as a caretaker or if you're doing any kind of healing work
- When dealing with people who can negatively affect you in any way

If you practice and make a conscious effort, in time you can transmute the energy of negativity. Instead of being affected by it, you can choose to send love to others who might be suffering. By protecting yourself from negativity you stay strong in your own energy; therefore, you have the ability to empower yourself and everyone around you.

PRAYER FOR PROTECTION FROM NEGATIVITY

Archangel Michael and my guardian angels, I have this situation _____ and I need your help. Please surround me in God's divine white light of protection (imagine a bubble of light surrounding you). Fill me with love and empower me with your strength and courage. Help me be centered in love and allow no negativity to enter my bubble. If any negativity comes my way, allow it to be transmuted into love and send it back out as waves of love to everyone involved. Thank you. I now feel safe and protected in your love.

When you are affected by negativity, you may have a physical reaction such as feeling shaky, drained, or even nauseous. You could also have an emotional reaction like anger, sadness, or distress. Mentally, you might feel confused or forgetful. All these reactions to negativity can be uncomfortable. The angels want to help you be at peace. Use this prayer to remove all negativity from your energy field. Notice how much better you feel after you invoke the assistance of Archangel Michael.

PRAYER TO RELEASE NEGATIVITY

Archangel Michael, please release me from all negativity and heal me right now. Release me from the negativity of others. Release my energy from anyone I am in fear of. (Imagine that everyone is unplugging from you and you are unplugging from others.) Archangel Raphael, God's healer, please restore my energy with green emerald healing light (imagine all your cells illuminating in green emerald healing light) and please send healing to all others involved. Thank you, Archangel Michael and Raphael, for your loving assistance.

PROTECTION FOR YOUR FAMILY

One of the most common fears people struggle with is the fear of losing someone they love. When panic sets in, the mind's imagination takes off like a small snowball being pushed from the top of a hill and becoming a giant snowball. For example, a family member is late coming home from work, and your mind jumps to the assumption that she is dead in a car accident. Or your child didn't call when he got to his friend's house, and your mind concludes that he's been abducted.

HOW MANY DO YOU NEED?

There is no limit to the number of angels you can call on for help. Call on 10,000 angels for protection if you feel you need them. They are waiting in multitudes ready to assist you in any way they can.

When fear begins to consume you, stop and call upon the angels of protection to help you and your loved ones. Immediately ask Archangel Michael, Archangel Zaphiel, and everyone's guardian angels to surround all those involved in love and protection. Choose to have faith and imagine them being embraced in the wings of the angels. See Michael and Zaphiel by their side. Ask the angels to release your fear and replace it with peace. Remind yourself to stay present in the moment where everything is okay. Call on the angels of protection in the following situations:

- When your loved one is late in coming home
- When a loved one is sick or not feeling well
- When your children are home alone and you're worried
- When your loved one is going through a challenging time and you can't be with him
- When your loved one is going through emotional issues and you don't know what to do
- When your loved one is traveling alone and you're worried for her safety

Recognize that your thoughts wander into the "what ifs" and acknowledge that you're worried and afraid. Seize the opportunity to shift your thoughts from fear into faith. Ask the angels for help and know that everyone involved will benefit when you shift your intention from fear to love.

Use the following prayer when you realize your thoughts are focused on fear and you need help from the angels of protection.

PRAYER FOR PROTECTION
FOR YOUR FAMILY

Guardian angels, Archangel Michael, and Archangel Zaphiel, please go to my loved ones (or say their name) right now. Surround them, protect them, and keep them safe. Help me release my fear so I can move into faith knowing that my loved ones are safe. Bless us all with peace and allow us to feel comforted and embraced in God's loving protection. Thank you.

It is not known precisely where angels dwell—whether in the air, the void, or the planets. It has not been God's pleasure that we should be informed of their abode.

—VOLTAIRE

SONG OF THE ANGELS
(WILLIAM-ADOLPHE BOUGUEREAU, C. 1881)

PROTECTION FOR YOUR HOME

Your home is your sacred dwelling place. You want your home to be filled with a positive, loving, and peaceful energy. When your home is filled with love, it feels light and happy and everyone feels comfortable and safe. If there is negativity in the home, you might feel heaviness in the air or you may feel uncomfortable being in the house. When this happens, call on the angels of protection and ask them to clear the energy in your home. Request that they remove all negativity so it feels peaceful once again.

Archangel Michael is the divine helper to call on for removing negativity from your home. You can also use this prayer for any space that needs clearing: your office, the building you work in, or even your car.

PRAYER FOR REMOVING
NEGATIVITY FROM YOUR HOME

Archangel Michael, please remove all negativity from this dwelling place. Please clear it from the foundation to the roof. When this is complete, please fill this space with love, light, and healing so all those who enter feel safe and peaceful. Archangel Michael, watch over my home and only send those who are good to its doors. Please ensure that harmony, love, happiness, and cooperation be the essence of our home. Thank you for your help.

Protecting Your Home

Fear can easily set in when you're home alone and your mind wanders to that scary movie or that dreadful story from the news. Before you know it, you're in the grip of fear. What if you could feel more peace when you're home alone? What if you could trust that your children or pets were being watched over when you're not at home? Imagine how good you would feel if you knew there was someone watching over your home twenty-four hours a day while you were on vacation. Whenever you are faced with any of these situations, call on Archangels Michael and Suriel to watch over your home and ask them to keep it safe from harm. God sent you these divine helpers so you could have peace and enjoy life, feeling safe wherever you are.

HOUSE ANGELS

Denise Linn, author of *Sacred Space* and a practitioner of feng shui, says that there are house angels who serve to protect the home. She says: "I believe that the most powerful guardian for your home is an angel. Calling upon the angels to be your house guardians for protection and spiritual rejuvenation can bring a wonderful feeling of peace, harmony, and safety to your home."

Use the following prayer before leaving your home and trust that the angels will do their job to watch over and protect both your home and any loved ones left behind.

PRAYER FOR PROTECTING YOUR HOME

I ask that four guardian angels stand watch at each corner of my home and property. I also call on Archangels Michael and Suriel to protect my home, its possessions, and all those who stay behind. Please help everyone feel safe and at peace knowing that our home is protected in the divine white light of God and the angels. Thank you.

PROTECTION FOR YOUR CAR

Your car is a place where you spend a significant amount of time, and you want to feel safe and secure no matter where you go. Think of the last time you felt vulnerable in your car. Maybe someone near you was driving recklessly. Maybe the weather conditions were poor, you got lost, or your car was experiencing mechanical difficulties.

Whenever these situations occur, it's time to call on the angels of protection. Imagine a beautiful radiant light surrounding your car. Ask the angels to keep your car and everyone in it safe. Ask that they stay with you until you arrive at your destination safely.

DON'T LET GO OF THE WHEEL!

Remember, it is always your job to be a responsible driver. The angels can help you if you are afraid or unsafe, but you will always need to be responsible before and after you get behind the wheel. Always follow the rules of the road.

Another time you can call on the angels of protection is when you need help driving the car itself. Imagine the angels sitting by your side in the passenger seat and ask them to help you stay alert so you can arrive at your destination safely. Another example might be when you're driving in bad weather and you feel afraid and doubt your ability to maneuver the car. Ask the angels to help you drive the car and ask for the courage and confidence you need. Also ask them to advise you if it's safer to pull over and wait out the storm.

Know that in any circumstance where you feel unsafe or afraid, it's time to call on the angels of protection. You can feel reassured that you are not alone and they are watching over you. Remember, everyone benefits when you feel safe and confident while driving your car.

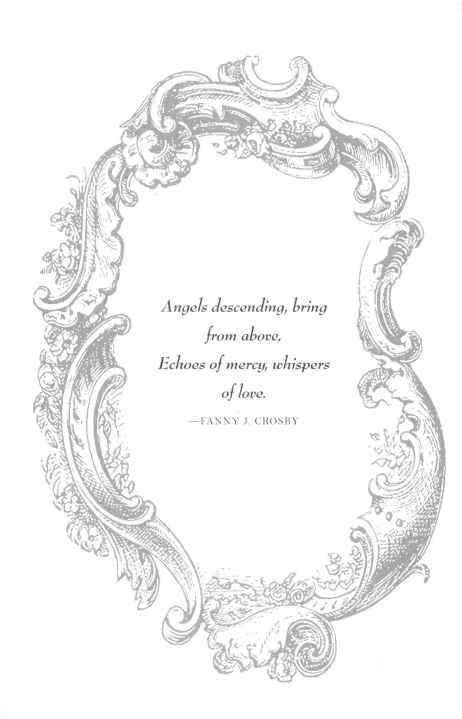

*Angels descending, bring
from above,
Echoes of mercy, whispers
of love.*

—FANNY J. CROSBY

CHAPTER TEN

Healing with the Angels

 f you require healing of any kind, reach out to the angels and ask for help. Healing means returning to a state of wholeness on every level—mind, body, and spirit. Discover how you can use the power of prayer to initiate your healing so you can become one with your true state of health and well-being.

ASKING FOR HEALING

Healing can take place on many levels and the angels can help you with all aspects of healing. The first step you need to take in order to initiate your healing process is to simply ask, "Angels, help me heal." Then be specific. Ask for the help you need and share with the angels how you want to feel when you are restored to full health and wholeness.

Try these examples of asking the angels for help with healing:

- **You are in physical pain.** Ask the angels to ease your pain and ask them to guide you to the resources you need (rest, doctors, healers, or medicine) in order to heal quickly and completely.
- **You are emotionally depressed.** Ask the angels for peace and the help you need to heal the source of your emotional pain.
- **You are struggling with relationship issues.** Ask the angels for healing so all involved experience harmony, peace, and cooperation.
- **You are mentally confused and forgetful.** Ask the angels for clarity so you can remember.
- **You feel alone and disconnected from God.** Ask the angels for spiritual healing so you can feel one with God and the angels.

A PRAYER TO INVOKE HEALING

Dearest angels of healing, please give me everything I need to heal completely. I am willing to heal on every level—mind, body, and spirit. I surrender and trust that you know exactly what I need and you will show me the way. I am paying attention and I commit to taking action on anything I must do in order to achieve wholeness.

After you ask the angels for help and you're specific about what you want, then you need to surrender and trust. The angels know how to help you heal as a whole person in mind, body, and spirit. It's not unusual for someone to need to heal emotionally before he can heal physically. For example, if Jack has a heart condition, the angels know he needs to release the stress in his life so that he can heal completely. They might arrange (behind the scenes) a few changes that can make Jack's life less stressful. A friend might offer the use of a vacation home, or a new job opportunity might suddenly appear— one that can provide a more relaxed lifestyle. This is exactly what he requires in order to heal and achieve full health and wholeness. So remember, when you ask the angels for healing, be willing to surrender and trust that you will be given exactly what you need in order to accomplish this, even if you don't recognize it right away.

The last step when asking the angels for help is your responsibility. Pay attention and take action on anything you receive intuitively or from outside resources. For example, let's say you've asked the angels to heal your depression and someone tells you about a meditation class. It's your job to pay attention and take action, knowing that your angels have sent you an opportunity to heal.

ANGELS OF HEALING

The following angels and archangels have the specific role of helping humanity heal. They help with healing of all kinds: physical, emotional, mental, spiritual, and healing for both humans and animals. Read about each one and see which of these divine helpers can help you in your life right now. Then use the prayers to invoke them into your life so they can help you heal.

The Master Healer

Raphael is the master healer, and he is committed to humanity, doing healing work of all kinds for mind, body, and spirit. He is known as the doctor archangel who brings healing both to humans and animals. You might see a green emerald healing light associated with Archangel Raphael's presence. He will come to all those who call on him and because he is an archangel, he can be with everyone simultaneously. If you are a healer of any kind, ask Archangel Raphael to guide you and assist you in your healing work. He wants to be of assistance to all those passionate about healing the world.

PRAYER TO ARCHANGEL RAPHAEL

Archangel Raphael, please surround me in your green emerald healing light. You are God's healer and therefore you have been given the power to heal for God. I request and accept divine healing on all levels: physical, emotional, mental, and spiritual healing. Show me and help me become one with the truth. I am healed, whole, and healthy. Thank you, Raphael, for this miracle of healing.

Emotional Healing

Zadkiel helps all those who call on him for emotional healing. He is known as the archangel of mercy and benevolence, and he wants humanity to let go of judgment and to accept each other with love, compassion, and understanding. If you are struggling with emotional issues of any kind, invoke the assistance of Zadkiel and ask him to intervene. Request that he heal your heart so you can feel compassion and forgiveness. Then ask for the healing to expand into your mind, body, and spirit so you experience emotional healing on all levels of consciousness.

PRAYER TO ARCHANGEL ZADKIEL

Archangel Zadkiel, I request your help for emotional healing. Help me release and dissolve any negative feelings toward myself and others. Help me heal and be free from the negative effects of judgment, unforgivingness, anger, and resentment. I am ready to heal with your help. Zadkiel, come into my heart and heal it so I can love myself and others and find peace once again.

Healing for Death and Grieving

Azrael's role is to comfort and assist the dying as they transition into the afterlife. He also watches over and helps heal all those grieving from a loss of any kind. If you know of someone who is close to death, send Azrael to her side and ask that she be eased of her suffering. If you are still grieving from a loss, ask Azrael to help heal your heart. He can also help you if you want to communicate with your loved one who has passed; just ask him to help you make that connection.

PRAYER TO ARCHANGEL AZRAEL

Archangel Azrael, we are suffering a loss of someone we love very much. Please help _____ have a smooth and peaceful transition back home to heaven. Please bring healing and peace to all those left behind and help them know that their loved one is at peace. If they want to communicate with their loved one, please help them connect and give them that miracle. Thank you for reminding us we are not alone and we are truly loved during these difficult times.

Healing of Addictions

Zerachiel is one of the seven archangels mentioned in the Book of Enoch. He is the angel of healing who watches over and helps all those suffering from addiction. He will also help all the children affected by parents with addiction. When you call on him you might feel warmth in your chest or tingling in your body. If you want to release an addictive behavior or if you know of someone who is suffering from addiction, call on Zerachiel and ask for his assistance.

PRAYER TO ARCHANGEL ZERACHIEL

Archangel Zerachiel, please help _____. She is struggling with this addiction and it's affecting everyone involved. I am asking for divine intervention to take place. Please bring healing to everyone, especially _____. Help her heal and find the courage and strength to stop and get the help she needs. Help her awaken to the desire to live a peaceful, healthy, and productive life where she rediscovers her worth and how loved she really is.

The archangels of healing will lovingly guide you along your journey to wellness. They know how hard it can be when you feel less than 100 percent both physically and emotionally. Call them by name and know that their role is to ease your pain and provide you with the peace you deserve so you can heal.

PHYSICAL HEALING

Your natural state of being is one of health and vitality. Do you remember the last time you were feeling sick and you had the flu or a cold? Now recall how good it felt and how grateful you were when you finally recovered.

Your body can be a wonderful messenger. If you are out of balance physically, mentally, or emotionally, disease will come knocking at your door trying to get your attention. Your body is telling you it's time to heal and take care of yourself. The angels of healing can help you do this and they want to assist you in bringing your body back into balance.

Whenever you're in pain or you're suffering from illness, call out to Archangel Raphael and the angels and ask them for physical healing. If you are in pain, ask them to relieve your pain so you can feel more peaceful. When you are sick or suffering from illness, ask them to give you everything you need so you can return to your natural state of health and well-being. Your job is to take responsibility for your health and follow your inner guidance so you can do what's necessary to heal yourself.

The angels of healing can help if you:

- Ask for the best medical care for your highest and greatest good.
- Ask for the patience you need to rest and heal.
- Ask for the emotional and mental healing you need to physically get better.

- Ask for the earth angels who can help you, and be willing to accept their help.
- Ask for any holistic or alternative approaches that will help you heal.
- Ask for any financial support you need to fund your healing process.
- Ask for a miracle.

The angels of healing can provide you with the support and resources you need to accelerate your healing process. When you are out of balance, surrender and trust that all is well. Your body and the angels are helping you remember that it's time to take care of yourself.

Use the following prayer whenever you are experiencing any kind of pain, sickness, or disease. Use it whenever you need it or until you feel healed, whole, and healthy.

PRAYER FOR PHYSICAL HEALING

Archangel Raphael and all the healing angels, please illuminate every cell in my being with green emerald healing light and restore my cells back to perfect health and wholeness. Give me everything I need to heal as a whole person: mind, body, and spirit. Provide me with the comfort, patience, and help I need so I can nurture myself back to full health. Thank you for the powerful healing and your loving support.

EMOTIONAL HEALING

Your emotional well-being is just as important as your physical health. When you are peaceful and content with your life, your body feels light, you take care of yourself, and you stay healthy. When you feel unfulfilled, depressed, and confused about your life, your body feels heavy, you don't take care of yourself, and you experience more sickness.

Throughout your life you will have many experiences, and emotional highs and emotional lows. Your health depends on how you process your emotions. Ask yourself, "Do I process my emotions in a healthy way or do I stuff them and bury them within?"

The angels of emotional healing can help you release and heal any toxic emotions that are affecting your life in a negative way. This can free you to experience more peace, joy, happiness, health, and overall well-being. The angels of emotional healing can help you. Here's how you can ask for help:

- When you notice painful emotions like sadness, anger, resentment, or hurt bubbling to the surface, call on the angels and ask for healing.
- Sit with the angels in prayer or meditation and ask them to help you heal. Share with them how you feel in the moment (you can always write about it) and then tell them how you want to feel.
- If you feel you need counseling or support of some kind, ask the angels to guide you to what you require in order to heal.
- Ask the angels to guide you to the perfect books, classes, or anything else you need that can bring you healing or new awareness.

- Before bed, ask the angels to help you heal during your dream state.
- Ask for a miracle and a feeling of inner peace.

The angels know you deserve peace and they want you to be happy. Allow them to guide you along your journey of emotional healing. They will be gentle, and God never gives you more than you can handle. Share with the angels of healing that you want to heal at a peaceful pace and ask them to give you everything you need in order to do so.

Use the following prayer whenever you are experiencing any kind of emotional pain such as sadness, depression, confusion, anger, jealousy, or resentment. Allow yourself to honor your emotions without judgment, knowing that the angels of healing are surrounding you and supporting you in unconditional love.

PRAYER FOR EMOTIONAL HEALING

Archangel Raphael, Archangel Zerachiel, and all my healing angels, please surround me and help me feel safe and supported in your loving presence. I am asking for emotional healing. I am feeling
_____. I know it's healthy for me to feel and heal these emotions, but I need your help. Please go to the root cause of my unsettling emotions and help me heal so I can feel _____.
Thank you, and please continue to give me everything I need for my highest and greatest good.

HEALING FROM ADDICTIONS

There are addictions of all kinds: food, drugs, alcohol, sex, and even work. An addictive behavior or habit can create disharmony and even destruction when it gets out of control. It can be very upsetting for friends and family members, and most of the time they feel helpless. If you or someone you know is suffering from an addiction of any kind, it's time to call on the angels of healing for help. No one has to feel alone in their struggle; the angels want to assist you and all those involved.

Take the following steps with the angels to heal an addiction:

1. Admit and share with the angels what your addiction is.
2. Ask Archangel Zerachiel and the angels of healing for help.
3. Ask for healing on all levels: physical, emotional, mental, and spiritual.
4. Ask for the people and resources you need to free yourself from addiction.
5. Take action to help yourself; reach out for help if you need it.
6. Watch for the signs. Continue to pray until you reach freedom.

JAOEL

Jaoel is an angel who helps with those seeking to overcome addiction. He is associated with Archangel Michael and his energy is very compassionate. He will help you overcome even the strongest resistance.

Whenever you have an addictive behavior or habit, it feels like it has control over you. The angels want you to know that you can experience freedom from this feeling of control. Trust in the power of God. Feel worthy and deserving and ask to receive this miracle of freedom. God and the angels want you to be healthy, happy, and peaceful.

PRAYER FOR HEALING FROM A PERSONAL ADDICTION

Archangel Zerachiel and the angels of healing, I am ready to receive your help and guidance so I can heal and be free of my addiction to _____. Please give me the courage, strength, and will to persevere until I feel free and peaceful with my choices and decisions. Please provide me with everything I need to move through this with support, love, and grace. Help me know that I am not alone and that I have a team of spiritual helpers guiding me. Thank you.

HEALING FOR THE DYING
AND GRIEVING

In countless angel stories, the dying and their family members describe the presence of angels or a visitation from a loved one. They come to the dying and their family members in hopes of reassuring them that they are being helped from the other side. Imagine the comfort you would feel if you knew the angels were by your side helping you or your loved one to transition from this world into the next.

CONNECTING IN SPIRIT

If you would like to connect with your loved one in spirit, ask Archangel Azrael to help you make that connection. You can ask for a visitation in your dreams or you can request to receive a clear and undeniable sign so you can be sure, beyond any doubt, that your loved one is okay and happy in heaven.

If you have a loved one who is dying, call on Archangel Azrael for help. His job is to comfort the dying and to help them when they're ready to cross over into heaven. Once they're in heaven he will stay with them, helping them make the transition as they adjust to their new surroundings. Be reassured that Azrael will make certain there is no suffering at the time of death, whether it's a sudden death or the person has been sick. He will also lend his support and provide healing for the grieving family members. Call on Azrael if you are grieving a loss of any kind and ask him to help you heal. Know that he will stay by your side until you transition through your loss and you feel peace again.

Use the following prayer whenever you want to send comfort and healing to the dying. You can also say this prayer if someone recently passed or they experienced a sudden or tragic death.

PRAYER FOR THE DYING

Archangel Azrael and the angels of healing, please surround _____ with your loving presence. Bring her comfort and peace and allow her to feel embraced and protected in God's love. Please watch over her and help her transition peacefully and smoothly into heaven.

Use the following prayer if you have experienced a loss of any kind or if you want to send prayers and comfort to others who are grieving.

PRAYER FOR GRIEVING

Archangel Azrael and the angels of healing, please come to me (or name the person you are praying for) now and comfort me. Help me heal the pain and sadness in my heart. Help me focus on the goodness and the blessings we've had. Give me the strength to move forward and find peace in my heart.

As you become more spiritually conscious, your angels and your soul will nudge toward healing. They know that in order for you to receive what you are praying for—peace, prosperity, relationships, health, and overall well-being—you need to heal what no longer serves you in your life. There is an abundance of support and love available to you, both on the spiritual plane and the earth plane. It's up to you to reach out and ask for help.

As you heal and accept more love, joy, and balance into your life, you will realize that you have the ability to create what you desire by healing from the inside out. The angels are elated to assist you along your healing journey. Call them by name or just call on the angels of healing and use the prayers to invoke their powerful healing abilities. Discover that you are not alone, and together with the angels you can create miracles.

I dreamt I saw an angel in the sky,
Her face was calm and fair up there on high;
She smiled at me—a strange and lovely smile
That had in it no thought of earthly guile.
She looked so fair, so strange and wondrous
    pure,
That 'twas an angel, I was passing sure;
She spoke—her voice was music in the air;
So sweet it was, it matched her person fair.
She asked me, "Is there aught that I can do?"
I humbly answered, "Make me fair as you."
She smiled again, that strange unearthly
    smile,
That made all mundane things seem crude
    and vile—
"Thou art not ready yet," she seemed to say
And with a sigh, she floated far away.

—DOROTHY S. SILVERMAN,
"THE ANGEL"

CHAPTER ELEVEN

Manifesting Your Dreams with the Angels

 hat if miracles were an everyday experience? Can you imagine how magical your life would be? The angels can deliver these miracles to you as long as you hold the belief that anything is possible. Together as a team, you and your angels can create your heart's desires. It's time to think outside of the box and step into the reality of heaven on earth. It's here and it's now and you can experience it with the help of the angels.

MANIFESTING WITH THE ANGELS

Manifesting is about creating what you want in your life and knowing you have the power to do it. It's no longer true that only the mystical saints and the "gifted ones" have this ability to perform magic or miracles. You have the power within you, and with the help of the angels you can manifest your dreams into reality. The following steps will help you own your power to manifest your true desires:

1. Get clear about what you desire. Make a wish list and release any limited thinking or negative beliefs while making your list. Believe that anything is possible.
2. Write positive affirmations, enhancing them with feeling and emotion. Claim what you desire now in the present moment.
3. Spend time in meditation visualizing what you truly desire. Match your visualizations with the feeling that it's already done.
4. Call on the angels and ask them to help you manifest your desires and then surrender your wishes to God and the angels.
5. Feel worthy and deserving and be open to receive your highest and best and the highest and best of all, better than you could ever imagine.

These steps are very powerful. You initiate a powerful energy by aligning your thoughts, beliefs, feelings, and visions to a desired outcome. This energy becomes the law of attraction, which draws to your reality the manifestation of what you requested.

THE LAW OF ATTRACTION

The simple definition of the law of attraction is "like attracts like" or as Proverb 23:7 says, "As a man thinks in his heart, so is he." It works like this: Your focused thoughts, feelings, and emotions are charged with energy or vibration, which acts as a magnet that attracts into your life exactly what you're focused on. So if your desire is to create prosperity but you're focused on thoughts of lack, then you will continue to experience situations that reflect lack. When you focus your intention and attention on thoughts and feelings of being prosperous while imagining yourself financially free, then you begin to draw to your reality a mirror reflection of this.

EMPOWER YOURSELF

Be kind to yourself as you reflect on the thought, "I am creating my reality." Be willing to take responsibility for what's not going right in your life and seek to change it. First, decide on a possibility that could bring you more peace and happiness and then ask the angels to empower you with everything you need to change it.

After you take this important action of owning your thoughts and feelings and matching them to your desires, then you need to let go of how it's going to happen or when it's going to happen. Release it to the angels and the universe and allow it to happen. Expect what you desire and then accept the miracle as it unfolds. Always pay attention, listen to your divine guidance, and take inspired action when it feels right. You will witness with gratitude the miracles of your manifestation coming into form. What was once a thought and a feeling will become your reality.

DIVINE MAGIC AND ALCHEMY

Divine magic is a magical occurrence as a result of divine intervention. Mysticism and mystical experiences have been a part of Judaism and the Kabbalah since the early days. The word "magic" has been widely misinterpreted throughout the ages. When you have the desire to learn about God and the connection of mysticism or magic to the divine, then you will discover the true meaning of divine magic. It is created and used from a loving intention as one chooses to co-create with the divine.

Alchemy is the power or process of transforming something common into something special. Have you ever heard alchemy described as "transmuting base metals into gold"? In medieval times, those who studied to be alchemists were dedicated to working on themselves in order for the process of alchemy to work. They often became hermits in their quest to pursue their desire. This desire came from the belief that if they recognized and became one with their full potential, then they could create from the power within and affect the transformation of matter. When you decide to realize your true potential as a divine being in a human body, you can become an alchemist in many ways.

When you ask the angels, they will teach you how to connect with divine power so you can experience divine magic and witness the process of alchemy. They will encourage you to own your power and use your natural gifts of divine magic and alchemy so you can live the life you were born to live—a life of happiness, joy, fulfillment, and peace.

ANGELS OF DIVINE MAGIC, MANIFESTATION, AND ALCHEMY

You deserve to have it all and to be happy in every aspect of your life. Work with the angels to create miracles and experience the power of divine magic. Down the road, when your dreams have come true, you will look back on your life and realize that the angels helped you get there. So start now and call on this team of angels so you can create your own experience of heaven on earth.

Divine Magic and Manifestation

Ariel is a healer of both the human and animal kingdoms. In the Kabbalah and Judaic mysticism, Ariel is associated with conducting divine magic and manifestation. Call on her to witness and experience the gifts of divine magic, so that together you can manifest what you desire.

PRAYER TO ARCHANGEL ARIEL

Archangel Ariel, I know you have the gift of divine magic and I ask for your help with the following desires and wishes (share with Ariel). Continue to show me all that I need to know so I can play my part in manifesting. Help me believe the impossible to be possible. Enhance my thoughts, feelings, and visions with positive divine energy so I can be empowered to manifest. Thank you, Ariel, for co-creating magic in my life.

Archangel Jeremiel Helps Manifest Your Heart's Desires

Jeremiel means "mercy of God" and in Judaism he is known as one of the seven core archangels. He is a visionary and he will help you manifest your dreams into reality. He will inspire you to reach for your highest goals and to hold your vision of what you desire until it comes true. He wants you to experience true happiness and will assist you in any way he can so you can create harmony in all aspects of your life.

PRAYER TO ARCHANGEL JEREMIEL

Archangel Jeremiel, you are the visionary, and with your help you can assist me in manifesting my true desires. Help me feel worthy and deserving of reaching my highest goals and my greatest potential. Help me believe in myself and the visions of my dreams (you can share some of your dreams with Jeremiel). Keep manifesting the miracles into my life so I can experience true happiness. Thank you, Jeremiel.

Archangel Raziel Helps with Divine Magic, Manifestation, and Alchemy

Raziel's name means "secret of God." He has this name because he knows all the secrets of the universe and how it works. All this secret knowledge and wisdom is recorded in *The Book of the Angel Raziel*, which is also considered a book of divine magic. Raziel is like a divine wizard and he can teach you about manifestation and working with the power of divine magic.

PRAYER TO ARCHANGEL RAZIEL

Archangel Raziel, you hold the secrets of the universe and you have the gift of divine magic. Teach me the wisdom of divine magic and help me manifest divine miracles into my life. Help me understand that when I am one with God anything can happen. These are the manifestations I would like help with right now in my life (share your desires). Thank you, Raziel, for sharing this secret knowledge.

Your Heart's Desires

Suriel is known as an angel of healing and an angel of death. Suriel will help you let go of limiting beliefs so you can manifest your heart's desires. He has the power to manifest anything from nothing. He will help you live your wildest dreams and experience heaven on earth.

PRAYER TO SURIEL

Dearest Suriel, you are an angel of healing and I ask you now to heal my limiting beliefs. You know better than I what holds me back from experiencing my heart's true desires. I am open and ready to experience my personal heaven on earth. Please help me believe so I can witness the miracles unfold and have my dreams manifest into reality. Thank you, Suriel, for all your help.

Divine Magic and Alchemy

Uriel brings illumination to all situations. In the Book of Enoch, Uriel is considered "one of the holy angels, who is over the world . . . the leader of them all." He is known for having the gift of prophecy and it was said that he warned Noah of the impending floods. Uriel has the knowledge of alchemy and he has the ability to manifest things out of thin air. If you want to learn about alchemy and the power of manifestation, call on Uriel and ask him to teach you and help you believe in the power of divine magic and alchemy.

PRAYER TO ARCHANGEL URIEL

Archangel Uriel, you carry the light of God and I ask you to illuminate the following situations in my life (share your desires). You have tremendous gifts of alchemy and divine magic and I am eager for you to teach me about these gifts. I am ready to experience the power of alchemy and divine magic in my life so I can manifest my true desires and intentions. Thank you, Uriel, for these gifts and for sharing your knowledge and wisdom.

As you can see, this is a team of angels who can help you manifest your true desires. Their role is to help you believe that anything is possible and that miracles really do happen. Take some time to pray and meditate with them and invoke them into your life so you can experience the magic of the divine.

CREATING THE EXPERIENCE OF HEAVEN ON EARTH

In the Bible, Matthew 6:10 says, "Thy kingdom come, Thy will be done in earth, as it is in heaven." It can be translated different ways, but what if it meant that the kingdom of heaven is already here and it's possible to experience heaven on earth? If this were true, you would be able to see and communicate with the angels, you would have everything you need, and the beauty and peace you imagine experiencing after death would be yours, right here and right now.

This might seem far-fetched to you in this moment, but wouldn't it be worth finding out if it's true? Notice how it feels to think about the possibility of experiencing heaven on earth. Imagine what it would be like if you were living the life of your dreams. Your relationships would be harmonious and loving, you would be in a job that you loved, you would live in a home that was filled with beauty and tranquility, your body would be healthy, your mind would be peaceful, your spirit would be alive, and there would be interconnectedness with all of humanity. The angels know it's possible and heaven on earth already exists all around you. Open your heart and your mind to experience the miracles waiting for you and ask the angels to help you live your personal expression of heaven on earth.

MANIFESTING YOUR HEAVEN ON EARTH

In heaven there is no time between a thought and its manifestation. When Jesus focused His thoughts on water, it transformed into wine instantaneously. This is the reality of heaven on earth. When you set your intentions and you focus your attention on your desires, they become your reality. The ultimate and most powerful place to be when you set your intentions is one with God, the Creator of all things.

HEAVEN IS ONENESS

"Heaven is not a place or a condition. It is merely an awareness of perfect oneness."—*A Course In Miracles*

Spend some time journaling or visualizing in meditation what your personal heaven on earth would look and feel like. What dreams and desires would you like to manifest in the following areas in your life?

- Relationships and family
- Body and health
- Emotional and spiritual well-being
- Job, career, or life purpose
- Financial
- Home
- Fun, travel, and creativity

After you are finished with your list, give it to the angels and say the following prayer:

Archangel Ariel, Archangel Jeremiel, Archangel Raziel, Suriel, and Archangel Uriel, I come to you sharing my dreams and desires. You are already one with God and have the power to create miracles. Help me become one with God and believe in the power of miracles and divine magic. I am open, I deserve, and I allow myself to experience heaven on earth in all aspects of my life. Deliver to me the gifts of manifestation and empower me to become a magnet so I can draw into my life everything I need to live my personal heaven on earth for my highest and best and the highest and best of all, better than I could ever imagine.

BECOME THE MAGNET OF YOUR DESIRES MEDITATION

Once you have created your wish list and surrendered it to the angels, you can do the following meditation to enhance and accelerate the law of attraction. As you raise your vibration and focus your energy on your desires with positive thoughts, feelings, and visualizations, you become a powerful magnet. Effortlessly, you attract everything you need to live your heart's desires and in a short period of time you will look back and realize what was once a thought became your reality.

MANIFESTATION MEDITATION

Take some quiet time and find a place where you will not be disturbed. Bring your wish list of your dreams and desires with you. Get comfortable and take a deep breath and let go of everything that happened before you closed your eyes. Then take another nice deep breath and let go of everything that's going to happen after you open your eyes. Now breathe into the present moment and believe that anything is possible when you open your heart and come into union with God and the angels. Now affirm to yourself and God that you are open to your highest and best and the highest and best of all, better than you could ever imagine.

With your eyes closed, ask Archangel Ariel, Archangel Jeremiel, Archangel Raziel, Suriel, Archangel Uriel, and any other angels to gather around you and ask for their help in manifesting your wish list. (Pause) Ask them to create a beautiful and sacred circle of divine light all around you. Know that in this circle, heaven on earth already exists and all the miracles you are asking for are already done. Imagine and feel the angels gather on the edge of the circle supporting you, loving you, and holding the energy of your sacred space. (Pause)

Start with the first area of your life you would like to manifest your dreams and desires. Imagine with as much feeling and emotion as you can that it's already done and you are experiencing it right now. (Pause) Now imagine yourself as a magnet and you are drawing to yourself everything you need to fulfill the manifestation of your desire. See or imagine the angels working behind the scenes making it all possible. Feel or imagine the magnetism of the energy field all around you, active and powerful. (Pause) After you finish with that area of your life, move to the next dream and desire and repeat the process.

When you have completed your wish list, affirm "and so it is" and thank the angels. This affirms your belief and faith in God and the angels. Trust in the power of the universal law of attraction and believe that miracles are on their way. Take a deep breath of gratitude and slowly and gently breathe yourself back into the present moment. Periodically look at your list and keep the feeling alive that you experienced in meditation until you are actually living it.

I dreamt a dream! what can it mean?
And that I was a maiden Queen,
Guarded by an Angel mild:
Witless woe was ne'er beguil'd!

And I wept both night and day,
And he wip'd my tears away,
And I wept both day and night,
And hid from him my heart's delight.

So he took his wings and fled;
Then the morn blush'd rosy red;
I dried my tears, and arm'd my fears
With ten thousand shields and spears.

Soon my Angel came again:
I was arm'd, he came in vain;
For the time of youth was fled,
And grey hairs were on my head.

—WILLIAM BLAKE,
"THE ANGEL"

CHAPTER TWELVE

Angel Stories and Miracles

ere are stories about divine intervention and the miracles people experience when they invite the angels into their lives, from a nine-year-old girl in a coma to a women dying of cancer. These stories will inspire you to invite the manifestations of miracles into your life and trust that the angels love you dearly and they want to help you in any way they can.

JEANNIE'S NEAR-DEATH EXPERIENCE

My story is a true experience that happened to me when I was a little girl, age nine. I was home sick for three days running a high temperature. When I got worse, my parents brought me to the emergency room. After the ER doctor saw me, he immediately sent me up to the operating room. I'll never forget when he said the word "stat." My appendix had ruptured and the doctor caught it just in time, right before it burst; however, the poison peritonitis set in. I was in a coma for a week and given my last rites.

During my time in a coma I took an amazing journey. I felt the love of God as my spirit left my body and I moved slowly through a tunnel of light. I was enveloped by divine light. It was like a warm red glowing sensation, a sensation of love. As I moved forward toward the light at the end of this tunnel, I could see all around me but I could also see me, if you can understand that. Pictures of my life were flashing before me in constant motion. With every picture of my life, good or bad, I could feel every feeling of that experience.

As I got closer to the end of the tunnel, I felt so happy. I was almost through the opening when I could see at the end a couple of white doves flying, a beautiful blue sky, and tall grass with flowers. It looked like heaven. The grass started parting as if it was welcoming me home and I felt love everywhere. All of a sudden I heard this deep voice behind me saying, "Go back, go back, your mother needs you." I didn't want to do any such thing. I was feeling love beyond what I could ever imagine, but the voice continued. I felt myself turning around (no body), and in the far distance I noticed a silhouetted person with no face, just a long robe. I listened to the voice and went back to my body in the hospital.

I woke up from my coma and about five weeks later I returned home. To this day, my mother has needed me both emotionally and financially. I know this was divine intervention, and to this day I still remember that voice. It reminds me of the important role I play in my mother's life and I will always be there for her.

I truly believe that each day is a blessing. Don't take it for granted. Thank God for your little miracles and blessings of each day. I do, and now have a second chance to make a difference.

ERIN'S MIRACULOUS DREAM

I was praying to the Blessed Mother Mary and Archangel Raphael, but mostly to Mary, about a friend of the family's little girl who was going through chemo and was running temps of 105°F and over. She couldn't battle the temperatures because her immune system was so low due to the chemo. So every time I thought of the little girl, I asked Mary and Archangel Raphael to help her and watch over her. This went on for four to five days. Then one night before I went to bed, I asked Mary again to help this little girl. I never remember my dreams, but this one I will never forget.

I was at my house when an angel came to see me. The angel took me to the hospital room of the little girl. I had never been to the hospital to see her because she was so sick and we didn't want to give her any germs to make her worse. When I got there, the whole room was filled with angels. So many were there that I didn't know how I was going to get in the room. Then the angels cleared a path for me so I could get to the bedside, where I saw Mary sitting beside the bed. Mary looked at me and said, "Don't worry, everything is going to be all right." I said thank you and I felt calmed. I woke up at this point and I felt very peaceful and went back to sleep.

When I woke up the next morning, I went and checked the website of the hospital where the family posted messages on how the little girl was doing. When I read it I got all filled up. It said that the little girl's fever broke and she was doing much better. One week later, the doctors took a spinal tap and some blood tests and shortly after we found out that the little girl is now in remission! Thank you, Mary, Archangel Raphael, and all the angels, for helping this little girl! She is home now from the hospital and doing much better! Thank you! Thank you!

NINETY MILES PER HOUR MIRACLE

When I lived in the mountains of New Mexico, I would occasionally go back and forth to the Dallas area of Texas to see my children and grandchildren. This was a thirteen-hour drive across eastern New Mexico and west Texas, the wide-open spaces of our country.

The temperature was around 100°F when I was returning home and I wanted to get back to my cool mountain home. I had been driving for about eight hours and going approximately ninety miles per hour. This speed is not unusual for that part of the country. I was approaching an eighteen wheeler and moved over to the left lane to pass. As I was about halfway into passing the truck, my right front tire exploded. It seemed as if time stood still. I could see the black pieces of the tire hitting the windshield. My thought was to try to pull over to the median on my left. I heard, "Don't touch the brakes. Don't touch the brakes. Keep the steering wheel steady!" I felt very calm, didn't touch the brakes, and kept the steering wheel steady. All of a sudden, I was stopped on the right side of the road and the truck was in back of me. How I got in front of the truck, I don't know. My first thought was to say thank you to all of the angels who helped me. My next thought was why? Why was I saved? I had to assume there was a reason.

By then, the truck driver was at my window asking me if I was okay. He said he couldn't figure out how I had got in front of him and off to the side of the road. He kindly replaced my front tire with the donut and I thanked him and off he went. The rest of the way home I continued to thank my angels and pondered the thought of why that all just happened.

THE EASY-BAKE OVEN MIRACLE

In 1997, I discovered the power of hypnosis to help me heal after being diagnosed with thyroid cancer. I believed in it so much that I wanted to get certified as a hypnotherapist. I found someone in my area who taught the certification course, but I put the brakes on and stopped myself from moving forward when I discovered the tuition fee was $1,200.

I could feel my soul nudging me to sign up for the course, but my fear set in and my bank account statement confirmed that I didn't have the money to pay for the course. So I sat down with my angels and I said to them, "If this is meant to be and it's in my highest and best to become a hypnotherapist, then show me the money."

A couple nights later my daughter asked me if she could use her Easy-Bake Oven that had been in the basement for over a year. I explained to her that she could get it from the basement, but I wasn't sure if there were any mixes left to make the desserts. When she brought the box up from the basement and I pulled out the oven, out came a check with it. It was a check, dated a year prior, that I never cashed from my sales commission, for $655.22. Not only that, the check was dated 11/11, which is a number which signifies the angels' presence. I called my boss and confirmed that I never cashed the check and he said he would gladly reissue it.

I followed the call of my soul, and with the help of the angels I signed up for the course and was certified as a hypnotherapist. The rest of the money came and by the end of the course I had paid it off in full.

After that experience, I framed the old check so I would never forget the truth—that the angels are watching over me and if I ask and it's meant to be, they will make it possible.

I MANIFESTED A SOUL PARTNER

After taking an eight-week course focused on the book *Excuse Me, Your Life is Waiting* by Lynn Grabhorn, I decided to work on manifesting my soul partner. I sat down with the angels and I made my wish list of what I really wanted in a relationship. I knew what I didn't want after experiencing my past relationship, and therefore I had more clarity about what I did desire.

I shared with the angels what I wanted to feel emotionally and physically with my partner. I asked for someone special who was spiritual, playful, supportive, financially secure, committed, honest, and open with communication. I allowed myself to ask for everything I wanted with no boundaries. My wish list was very detailed and it included our future family life, our home, travel plans, and shared interests as we got older. After three days of working on my wish list, I completed it by including my prayers of surrender to God and the angels. I prayed that my soul partner would enter my life for the greatest good of all, better than I could ever imagine.

Three weeks later he walked into my life. It took me a while to figure out that it was him, but once I did, I went back to my wish list and I checked everything off on my list. My angels listened, and it was worth the three days I spent getting clear about what I wanted and what I deserved. It's been seven years now and it's better than I could have imagined.

DONNA'S SIGN FROM HER ANGEL

I was diagnosed in March with inflammatory breast cancer. After undergoing chemo, a mastectomy, and radiation, I am doing very well! A few weeks ago I went for my first mammogram. You can only imagine how scared I was. I had prayed to my angel the day before to please show me a sign of a star so I would know that she was around me. After having the mammogram *three* times, the third time I just burst into tears, thinking the cancer was now in my other breast, the radiologist came in to tell me that everything was fine.

When we got off the elevator to go to our car, the parking attendant saw us, and he took something off the hood of our van. As we walked closer to him, he held something out to us in his hand and asked, "Is this yours?" It was a little charm, a *star*! I just stood there with my mouth open in shock. My husband responded, "I guess so." I shared with him my prayer about asking my angel for a sign of a star and he was just amazed. I guess that was my angel letting me know that she was with me throughout that whole thing! I feel so blessed!

ARCHANGEL MICHAEL THE FIREFIGHTER

This story is a wonderful illustration describing the role of Archangel Michael. He is the protector and he will watch over you, your loved ones, and your home. Pamela's story is also a great example of how your intuition, or your angel's, might try to get your attention before something occurs in the near future.

One night, I was going through my angel card decks looking for an Archangel Michael card. I have several decks, and after looking through all of them I was drawn to one in particular. The picture of him was so beautiful, his wings were stunning. I made a color copy of it and returned it to my room. I sat staring at the card and quickly fell asleep.

At 11:00 P.M., my oldest son, Wally, came running into my room saying, "The candle's on fire!" He had come upstairs for something to drink and he saw the candle in the living room out of the corner of his eye. It was not something he could simply blow out. It was a fairly good size candle in a clay pot. The wax was boiling and the entire surface was in flames. We went back in the living room and with great effort we put out the fire. The candle was on our computer desk and the shelf above the candle was black with soot and starting to singe.

When things calmed down, I sat down at my kitchen table, speechless. I sat in silence for a very long time. The reality of how close we came to having a major house fire was more than I could take in. We had been just seconds away from a major disaster. But nothing happened.

I eventually went back to my room and again looked at the Archangel Michael card and it reads: "YOU ARE SAFE" Archangel Michael, "I am protecting you against lower energies, and guarding you, your loved ones, and your home."

I had my answer and I knew Archangel Michael was watching over and protecting us. Thank you, Michael, and also thank you to my son for following his divine guidance.

AN ANGEL ON THE EDGE OF A CLIFF

When my sister and I were little girls, maybe eight or nine years old, our parents took us to New Hampshire for vacation. My mom decided we should visit the Flume. It's a very beautiful, very old passage, carved into the rock by the water. You climb and climb until you reach the top, where you can look back and see an amazing view. As we reached the top, my parents stopped to talk and my sister and I walked approximately twenty feet away from them. We were on a round overlook that jutted out over the steep edge of the Flume. It was completely surrounded by a two-rail wooden fence.

She and I stood together looking over the top rail. To get a better view, I stood on the bottom rail and held onto the top one. I can still remember how the damp wood felt against my hand. Suddenly, I lost my footing and slid between the top and bottom rail. I instantly found myself on my back, sliding down the cliff. I heard my sister scream as I reached over my head and caught the bottom rail with my hand. I was completely terrified and could feel the earth slipping below my feet. In that same moment, I felt a hand grab me by my wrist and pull me back up to safety. My sister saw the man who saved me. She watched as he pulled me to my feet. My sister and I hugged for a moment and turned to speak to my hero. He somehow vanished as quickly as he arrived. As we looked back, we saw my parents in the exact spot we left them and there were a few other people standing at the rail. None of them had seemed to move. When we explained to our parents what happened, they told us we should be more careful, but they also couldn't find the man who grabbed my wrist to thank him.

I'm not sure if my sister and I used the term angel on that day, but even as small girls we knew that whatever happened, it was profound, magical, and life-changing. Now as women, we sometimes reflect back on that event, knowing that we were not only blessed by the presence of an angel but we had each other to witness the experience together.

BEBE JOEY AND THE TINY SHAMROCK

My daughter Brenda was two months pregnant. Blood tests indicated that she may not have a viable pregnancy. My son-in-law, Joe, was unfazed by the tests. He was convinced that all was well. Joe is blonde, blue eyed, and a huge Boston Celtics fan. Being a nurse, I knew that the outcome was very uncertain. I was worried about my daughter and her unborn child. I asked my angels for a sign that all was well.

Later that day I was in a gift shop, not looking for anything in particular, just sort of browsing around. I looked down and there was my sign. On the shelf in a beautiful gold box was a newborn onesie. It was pure white and its only decoration was a tiny green shamrock. The tag read "Bebe Joey." I was filled with relief and gratitude and cried as I paid for that beautiful white onesie with its tiny shamrock. Seven months later, blonde, blue eyed, baby Joey wore that onesie home from the hospital.

BETHANEY'S MIRACLE OF HEALING AND FORGIVENESS

For the past two weeks I have been working with the angels of healing and forgiveness. My husband and I had a wedding this past Saturday for his cousin, and it was an uncomfortable and difficult situation for us. There is major anger and fighting in the family. We contemplated not attending the wedding, but we decided to be there to support his cousin. Since I was working with the angels of healing and forgiveness, I called on them specifically for this day. I asked them to be with the entire family and I prayed for peace. My husband and I set the following intention for the wedding: To support his cousin and his new wife.

To make a long story short, after the wedding and during the reception there were tears, apologies, and talk of regret. It was crazy! We were caught completely off guard and my husband was dumbfounded.

After the wedding, we were invited to an after-party and we decided to go, to further the healing process and to speak our peace. We called on the angels again, especially Archangel Michael and Archangel Gabriel, for courage and clear communication to speak our truth. I reminded my husband that there was also an opportunity for him to heal as well as his family. He opened up to the opportunity so he could let go of his anger, move toward forgiveness and have compassion for others' pain as well. And he did; it was so amazing! The healing for all was incredible! We are grateful to be taking these steps forward. It was miraculous! Today we feel freer and we are experiencing more peace than we have had in a long time.

A GIFT OF GRACE

This story is about a young woman, twenty-four years old, and a friend of the family who was dying from a brain tumor.

I am an occupational therapist and I worked with Cheryl since her evaluation at the hospital where I worked on 9/11/01 (a bad day for many reasons). I worked with her weekly until she died on February 2, 2008.

The night before she died, I was asked by the family to bring a splint over for her left hand because it was painful and it needed support. The patient at this point was nonverbal and clearly in need of "going home." Her eyes said more to me than any conversation I had with her the past fifteen years since I've known her. It was very clear to me that she didn't want to let her parents down and die. I knew her parents had to be told to "allow" her to go. As I was walking from their family room to the front door to leave, a very clear voice in my head said, "Tell them. You must tell them!" It was gentle but firm and absolutely unmistakable who it was. I was thinking in my head, "I cannot do that, I cannot tell these people to let their daughter die." There was now fifteen feet between me and the door. I had to make my decision as the voice got louder and firmer. As I walked to the door, many thoughts went through my head. These folks were long-standing family friends as well as business associates. What could I possibly say? What right did I have to tell these parents, "Let your beloved daughter die?"

As I turned to say goodbye at the door, I looked directly in the mother's eyes. When I opened my mouth to speak, I had no idea what would come out. The voice made one last pitch, "TELL

HER." I simply said, "It's time for Cheryl to go home." I waited for her mom to whack me and throw me out the door. Instead, she just collapsed in my arms and sobbed. I then said, "You must tell her it's all right to go home." As she agreed, still hugging and thanking me, I thought, "Where did that voice come from?" I then turned and left the house. As the door closed behind me, I heard that voice say, "Well done." I sobbed all the way home. Cheryl died the next day after her parents told her she fought a good fight and they were proud of her.

Later, when I thought about this profound experience, I realized that all those Sundays I went to Cheryl's home to work with her were not for her at all. They were, in fact, for me. All those Sundays prepared me to be at Cheryl's home at that exact moment in time, to listen to the voice and follow those instructions with faith. I recognized that I had heard that divine voice many times in my life. I chose this time to listen. I have been listening ever since.

THE ARCHANGELS AND THE ANGELS

ARCHANGELS

NAME	MEANING OF NAME	TYPE OF ASSISTANCE
Archangel Ariel	"lion or lioness of God"	Protecting the environment, animals, and the waters, protection if you travel by water, helps with sick or lost pets, relationship harmony, divine magic, and manifestation
Archangel Azrael	"whom God heals"	Comforting the dying and grieving, helps with transition from this life into the afterlife, helps you communicate with loved ones who have passed
Archangel Chamuel	"he who seeks God"	Finding lost items, healing of the heart, compassion, relationship healing including forgiveness, finding true love, enhancing your current relationship, career, and life purpose
Archangel Gabriel	"God is my strength"	Clear communication with God, life purpose involving the arts, adopting a child, fertility or child conception, communicating with spirit or your unborn child

NAME	MEANING OF NAME	TYPE OF ASSISTANCE
Archangel Haniel	"glory of the grace of God"	Grace, meeting new people and creating new friendships, finding true love, discovering and enhancing your spiritual gifts, developing clairvoyance and your psychic abilities
Archangel Jehudiel	"laudation of God"	Divine direction, building self-esteem and confidence, getting a job
Archangel Jeremiel	"mercy of God"	Manifesting your heart's desires, creating your best future, understanding prophetic information, understanding and interpreting your dreams, and life reviews to take an inventory of your life
Archangel Michael	"he who is like God"	Protecting children, protection during travel, protection of all kinds, mechanical difficulties, patron saint of policemen, releasing and shielding from negativity, chakra clearing, courage, strength, self-esteem, motivation, direction, and life purpose
Archangel Raphael	"God heals" or "God has healed"	Healing of all kinds, animals, protecting travelers, protects and watches over pets

NAME	MEANING OF NAME	TYPE OF ASSISTANCE
Archangel Raziel	"secret of God"	Divine magic, manifestation, alchemy, abundance, prosperity, spiritual growth, enhancing psychic abilities, understanding esoteric information, and sharing the wisdom of the universe
Archangel Sariel	"light of God"	Creating loving relationships, healing and enhancing relationships, guidance in your dreams, and interpreting your dreams
Archangel Uriel	"God is light" or "fire of God"	Weather, prophecy, bringing light to a situation, manifestation, divine magic, and alchemy
Archangel Zadkiel	"the righteousness of God"	Healing guilt, emotional healing, releasing judgment, healing with acceptance and compassion, and helps with forgiveness for self and others
Archangel Zaphiel	"God's knowledge"	Protecting and watching over children, healing of the heart, forgiveness of self and others, healing anger, and weather conditions
Archangel Zerachiel	"God's command"	Finding lost items, healing addictions, and helping children affected by parents of addiction

ANGELS

NAME	MEANING OF NAME	TYPE OF ASSISTANCE
Barakiel	"God's blessing"	Good fortune, abundance, maintaining a positive outlook and encouragement
Bath Kol	"daughter of voice"	Forgiveness of self and others and healing of the heart
Gadiel	"God is my wealth"	Releasing negativity, abundance and prosperity, finding life direction, transforming disagreements into compassion and forgiveness
Gamaliel	"recompense of God"	Miracles, experiencing more joy and happiness, gifts of all kinds, abundance and prosperity
Gazardiel	"the illuminated one"	Finding a new career, getting a raise, illuminates your path ahead, and opportunities
Hasmal	Known as the fire-speaking angel who guards the throne of God	Releasing limiting beliefs, discovering your divine purpose, and creating your highest potential
Laylah	An angel of the night; his name comes from the Hebrew word meaning sleep	Watching over newborn children and new mothers

NAME	MEANING OF NAME	TYPE OF ASSISTANCE
Pathiel	"the opener"	Opening the gates to manifestation, abundance and prosperity, wishes and desires, and computer problems
Suriel	the angel who rules over the earth	Protecting your home and possessions, manifesting your heart's desires, letting go of your limiting beliefs, experiencing heaven on Earth

INDEX

Hollingsworth, Paul
M., 1932-

Elementary teaching
methods.

$37.91

MAR 1 7 1992

DATE		